TEACH YOURSELF BOOKS

CONTRACT BRIDGE

For many years Patrick Cotter has been a prominent and established figure in bridge. Twice winner and four times finalist of the Gold Cup, the British Championship, he is also the winner of many other tournaments. He has represented England in the Home Internationals and Great Britain in the European Championship, and is at present bridge correspondent of both the *Financial Times* and *Country Life*. Patrick Cotter is also an international croquet player, three times winner of the Open Championship and winner in 1956 of the World Doubles Championship. He is the author of several books on bridge and croquet and was a Scholar of both St. Paul's School, London, and Christ Church, Oxford.

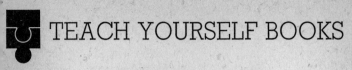

TEACH YOURSELF BOOKS

CONTRACT BRIDGE

E.P.C. Cotter

Bridge Correspondent of the *Financial Times*
and *Country Life*

ST. PAUL'S HOUSE WARWICK LANE LONDON EC4P 4AH

First printed 1969
Second edition 1975

ISBN 0 340 19500 2

Printed in Great Britain for The English Universities Press Ltd by Fletcher & Son Ltd, Norwich and bound by Richard Clay (The Chaucer Press) Ltd, Bungay, Suffolk

CONTENTS

PREFACE

Though the original idea was to revise Mr. Hartley's book which was the first on Bridge in this series, I felt on reading through his book that it was out of date and rather more diffuse than an instructional book should be. I have, therefore, completely rewritten it, though I have to a large extent kept to the original chapter headings.

As I have mentioned in the text this book will quickly make the beginner a reasonably good bidder, if the principles laid down are understood and put into practice, but to become a proficient player of the cards needs experience in the fight. The written word can put you on the right lines and show the logic that lies behind good card-play, but it is the mistakes you make at the card table, provided that you are humble enough to learn from them, that will provide the true instruction needed for your progress.

E. P. C. COTTER

London, 1969

1

CONTRACT BRIDGE—AN INTRODUCTION

BRIDGE is one of the most popular games ever invented, and gives pleasure to millions of people throughout the world. If I had to choose the best game, my vote would go to Bridge. And I say this as one who has taken part in many games at championship or tournament level. Bridge may lack the appeal of an outdoor sport, but *as a game* it is second to none. Furthermore, it is governed by good laws. There is no referee to penalise the late tackle, no umpire to uphold or reject an appeal for l.b.w., no linesman to decide that a service return is out. It is the players themselves who uphold the laws, laws which are designed to define the game, not to cater for unfair practices. Bridge has one answer to the player who deliberately breaks the laws in order to get some advantage, and that is ostracism.

As Bridge is a good game it is worth playing well. This is something that you owe to yourself, for it is man's nature to express intelligence, and Bridge gives you a real opportunity to do this. It is also something that you owe to your partner, for Bridge is a partnership game, and to be a good partner is worth more than all burnt offerings. Many skilful players fail to reach the top because they lack the ability to be good partners.

This book is designed to start you on the right lines. If you make a real effort to understand the principles of bidding that are laid down and put them into practice, you will soon be looked upon as a player whose bids can be trusted, for these principles can to a large extent be learned from a book. But this book will not send you forth as a proficient player of the cards. This is something that is beyond the powers of the written word, as I have stated in the chapter on The Play of the Cards. It will, however, give you a basis on which to work and something to which you can refer, as your practical experience makes you more alive to the problems that face the dummy player and the defender, and more anxious to overcome them.

PRELIMINARIES

The Game

Contract Bridge is a game played with one pack of playing cards.

Players

Bridge is a game for four players; two, sitting opposite each other, constituting a side against the other two. Thus "North" and "South" play against "East" and "West".

Equipment

A table, four chairs, two packs of cards, four scoring pads and pencils.

Pack of Cards

A pack of cards consists of fifty-two cards divided into four suits, each of thirteen cards.

The Suits

The suits and their symbols are:

Spades (♠), Hearts (♡), Diamonds (◇), Clubs (♣).

Spades and Hearts are called Major suits, Diamonds and Clubs are called Minor suits.

Rank of Suits

The suits rank (for bidding purposes) in the above order, Spades being the highest, Clubs the lowest.

The Cards

Each suit consists of thirteen cards that rank in the following order:

Ace (highest), King, Queen, Knave, Ten, Nine, Eight, Seven, Six, Five, Four, Three, Two.

The five highest cards, Ace (A), King (K), Queen (Q), Knave (J) and Ten, are called Honour Cards. The Knave is also called the Jack, hence the abbreviation J.

Drawing for Partners

One pack of cards is spread out face downwards on the table. Each player draws one card. When all four have drawn, the four cards are turned face upwards. The two highest play against the two lowest. If the four cards drawn are the Seven of Diamonds, the King of Clubs, the Three of Clubs and the Ten of Spades, the King and Ten play against the Seven and Three.

If two or more cards of the same rank are drawn, the rank of the suits determines the precedence. If the four cards drawn are the Ace of Spades, the King of Hearts, the King of Diamonds and the Two of Clubs, the Ace of Spades and the King of Hearts play against the King of Diamonds and the Two of Clubs.

Drawing the Highest Card

The highest card drawn confers upon the player drawing it three privileges:

1. The first deal.
2. The choice of cards. He may choose which pack (say Red or Blue) he wishes to deal.
3. The choice of seats. He may choose which of the four seats he wishes to occupy. When he has chosen, his partner must sit opposite, one opponent must sit on his right, the other on his left.

The Shuffle

The player on the dealer's left takes the cards chosen by the dealer, shuffles them and places them face downwards on his right. The dealer then picks them up, may shuffle them himself if he wishes, and places them on his right for his right-hand opponent to cut.

The Cut

The right-hand opponent divides the pack into two portions, lifting off the top of the pack not fewer than four nor more than forty-eight cards, and placing this portion beside the lower portion on the table.

Completing the Cut

The dealer completes the cut by placing the lower portion on top of the upper portion. The dealer is now ready to deal.

The Deal

The dealer distributes the cards face downwards, one at a time, to each player, starting with the left-hand opponent and proceeding in a clockwise direction until all fifty-two cards are dealt.

Picking up the Dealt Cards

When all the cards have been dealt, and *not before*, each player picks up the thirteen cards in front of him. These constitute his "hand".

The Second Pack and Rotation of Deal

While the dealer is dealing the Blue pack, his partner should shuffle the Red pack and place it face downwards on his right ready for the next deal.

The deal passes in turn to the player on the left of the previous dealer. Thus if South deals the first hand, West deals the second, North the third and so on.

Sorting the Hand

To enable a player to see clearly what he has been dealt, he should sort his hand into suits and arrange each suit in ranking order. It is also helpful to alternate red and black suits.

·The four players, each holding thirteen cards, are now ready to play a game of Bridge. What they do will be discussed in the next section.

THE AUCTION AND THE PLAY

Each hand is divided into two parts, the Auction, which is a tender for Contract, and the Play, which is fulfilment of Contract.

As it is the Auction that decides which player is to be Declarer and play the hand, it must take place before the Play begins. Now the Bridge player, though he is ultimately bidding for *points*, is at the beginning more like a contracting engineer making a tender for a project such as a highway fly-over. He must have the necessary qualifications and financial backing before he can even think of making a tender. There is a rival firm, represented by his opponents, in the market, and if their assets are greater than his then they are going to secure the contract.

The Bridge player does not bid for points, but he offers to deliver (win) a certain number of Tricks. The Contract goes to the side making the highest bid. If this side is able to fulfil its obligations its Tricks become realizable assets in the shape of points. But if the side is unable to make good its promise there is legal machinery to penalize it for its defaulting.

Before we go any further into the question of bidding, there are a few technical terms that must be explained.

Tricks

There are four cards in a Trick, each player contributing one. It is clear that there are thirteen Tricks in every hand or deal.

The Book

The first six Tricks that the declarer wins constitute the Book, and they do not count towards his score. When a player bids One in any denomination he is in reality contracting to win the odd Trick over the Book, or seven Tricks in all. Similarly, if he bids Seven he is contracting to win all thirteen Tricks.

Trumps and No Trumps

When a player makes a bid he must either name one of the four suits as trumps or specify another denomination known as No Trumps.

The word "trump" is connected with the word "triumph" and the trump suit can triumph over the other suits, so that the lowly Two of the trump suit can capture the lordly Ace of another suit. This precedence of the trump suit is subject to the rule of "following suit", which you will learn about later.

If a player specifies No Trumps it means that he does not want to have any suit as trumps.

You have learnt about the order in which the suits rank for bidding purposes, *but No Trumps outranks any suit*.

The Bid or Call

A bid is a tender for a specified number of Tricks.

A call is any bid, No Bid, Double or Redouble.

Each player in turn, starting with the dealer, is entitled to make at least one bid or call. No player is obliged to make a positive tender—he can always say No Bid.

If all four players say No Bid, there is no tender and so no fulfilment of Contract. The deal is at once abandoned, and the next player in rotation deals with the other pack.

The dealer may call No Bid, or name any number from One to Seven in No Trumps or in a suit.

The next player, and each player in turn thereafter, may call No Bid, or name any number in No Trumps or in a suit, provided that his bid names either a greater number of Tricks than the last bid or an equal number in a denomination of higher rank.

Double and Redouble

There are two other calls which can occur during the Auction. Any player may, in his turn, double the last bid if it was made by an opponent. As a Double increases the premiums and penalties for the Declarer, according to the success or failure of his contract, it does, in effect, challenge the Declarer's ability to meet his liabilities.

Any player may, in his turn, redouble the last bid if it was made by his own side and has been doubled by an opponent.

Termination of the Auction

The Auction terminates when any bid, Double or Redouble is followed by three consecutive calls of No Bid.

Let us take an imaginary Auction as follows:

South deals and bids One Spade, West says Two Clubs, North says No Bid, East bids Two Diamonds. On the second round of bidding South says Three Spades, West says No Bid, North bids Four Spades, East says No Bid. On the third round South says No Bid and West says No Bid. That ends the Auction as there have been three consecutive No Bids or passes.

Let us examine the bidding in detail. South, by bidding One Spade, undertakes to win for his side Seven Tricks with Spades as trumps. West says Two Clubs—he cannot say One Club because Clubs rank below Spades—thereby promising to win eight Tricks. North passes, and East suggests an alternative eight-Trick Contract in Diamonds. It is sufficient for him to call Two Diamonds because Diamonds outrank Clubs. South now calls Three Spades. Two Spades would have been enough, but South wants to show a good hand by offering to make nine Tricks. West passes, but North, though he has previously said No Bid, feels justified in bidding for ten Tricks, which as you will learn later is enough for Game.

It will be good for you to see the above bidding sequence written out in Bridge abbreviation.

S	W	N	E
1 ♠	2 ♣	No	2 ♢
3 ♠	No	4 ♠	No
No	No	—	—

What has emerged from this Auction? Two things have been determined:

The Contract and the Declarer

The Contract (*or* Final Contract) is the highest bid of the Auction, and the side making the final bid becomes the Declaring Side.

The Declarer is that member of the Declaring Side who *first* named the denomination of the Contract.

If we refer to the bidding table above we shall see that the highest bid was made by North, so that the Contract is Four Spades. North and South therefore become the Declaring Side. The Declarer, however, is South, because he was the first to name the denomination Spades.

This brings us to the point where the Play begins.

The Defending Side

The opponents of the Declarer are known as the Defending Side or the Defenders.

Lead to the First Trick

The Declarer's left-hand opponent makes the first lead. He may lead any card that he chooses.

Dummy

As soon as the opening lead has been made the Declarer's partner lays his cards face upwards on the table in front of him. He is known as Dummy, and takes no active part in the Play. The Declarer plays both his own hand and the Dummy.

Play to a Trick

After a card has been led by the Leader to a Trick each of the other three players, in strict clockwise rotation, must play a card to complete the Trick. He must "follow suit" if able to do so; that is, he must play a card of the same suit as the Lead. If he has no card of the suit led he is free to play any card that he may hold.

Winning of Tricks

Each Trick is won by the highest card *of the suit led*, unless there is a trump suit, when it is won by the highest trump.

Lead to subsequent Tricks

To all Tricks subsequent to the first Trick the lead is made by the winner of the previous Trick.

Termination of Play

Play continues until all thirteen Tricks have been completed.

Let us now play through an imaginary hand and see the mechanics of Leads and Tricks. Here is the hand set out in the usual diagrammatic form:

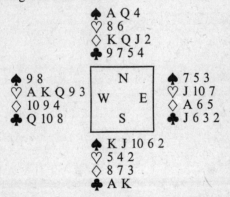

The Contract is Four Spades. The Declarer is South.

Trick 1

West leads because he is the left-hand opponent. He leads the Ace of Hearts (♡ A) and North faces his cards.

South, playing both hands, plays the Six of Hearts from dummy (♡ 6).

East plays the Seven of Hearts (♡ 7).

South plays from his own hand the Two of Hearts (♡ 2).

Notice that North, East and South hold Hearts in their hands so they are obliged to play them.

A player must play a card of the same suit as the Lead if able to do so.

The trick is won by West with the Ace—one Trick to the Defenders.

Trick 2

West leads because he is the winner of the previous Trick.

He leads ♡ K, and North, East and South follow with ♡ 8, ♡ 10 and ♡ 4.

West wins the Trick with the King—two Tricks to the Defenders.

Trick 3

West, still the leader, leads ♡ Q.

North, having no more Hearts, is free to play any card. He plays ♠ 4.

East and South follow with ♡ J and ♡ 5.

North wins the Trick with ♠ 4, because he has played a trump which "takes" a card of any other suit—one Trick to the Declarer.

Trick 4

North leads ♠ A, and East, South and West follow with ♠ 3, ♠ 2, ♠ 8.

North wins—two Tricks to the Declarer.

Trick 5

North leads ♠ Q. East, South and West follow with ♠ 5, ♠ 6, ♠ 9.

North wins—three Tricks to the Declarer.

Trick 6

North leads ♣ 4, East plays ♣ 2, South plays ♣ K, West plays ♣ 8.

South wins—four Tricks to the Declarer.

Trick 7

South leads ♠ K, West plays ♡ 3, North plays ♣ 5, East plays ♠ 7.

Neither West nor North are able to follow, but as it is the trump suit that has been led the cards that they discard cannot affect the winning of the Trick.

South wins—five Tricks to the Declarer.

Trick 8

South leads ♢ 3, West plays ♢ 4, North plays ♢ J, East plays ♢ A.

East wins—three Tricks to the Defenders.

Trick 9

East leads ♣ 3, South plays ♣ A, West plays ♣ 10, North plays ♣ 7.

South wins—six Tricks to the Declarer.

Trick 10

South leads ♢ 7, West plays ♢ 9, North plays ♢ Q, East plays ♢ 5.

North wins—seven Tricks to the Declarer.

Trick 11

North leads ♢ K, and the other players follow.

North wins—eight Tricks to the Declarer.

Trick 12 and 13

These Tricks must be won by South as he has the only two trumps left—ten Tricks to the Declarer.

The result of the hand is that the Declaring Side have won ten Tricks and the Defending Side have won three Tricks. North and South have made their Contract and score 120 below the line (see next section).

Contract Bridge Scoring Table

TRICK POINTS

Suit Bids	♠	♡	◇	♣	No Trumps Bids	
					First Trick	Sub-sequent Tricks
Each Trick bid and made	30	30	20	20	40	30
if doubled	60	60	40	40	80	60
if redoubled	120	120	80	80	160	120

Game is 100 Points, made up of Trick Points

PREMIUM POINTS

Undertricks	Not Vulnerable	Vulnerable
Each Undertrick Counts	50	100
If doubled		
First Undertrick counts	100	200
Subsequent Undertricks count	200	300
If redoubled		
First Undertrick counts	200	400
Subsequent Undertricks count	400	600

A side that has scored one Game is said to be *vulnerable*

BONUS POINTS

	Not Vulnerable	Vulnerable
1. Overtricks		
Each Trick made over Contract	Trick value	Trick value
if doubled	100	200
if redoubled	200	400
2. Fulfilment of doubled or redoubled Contract	50	50
3. Slams		
Small Slam bid and made	500	750
Grand Slam bid and made	1000	1500
4. Rubber		
If opponents win no Game	700	
If opponents win one Game	500	
For one Game in unfinished Rubber	300	
For part-score in unfinished Game	50	

HONOUR POINTS

For holding Four Honours of the Trump Suit in one Hand 100
For holding Five Honours of the Trump Suit in one Hand 150
For holding Four Aces at No Trumps in one Hand 150

THE OBJECT OF THE GAME

At cricket the object of the batting side is to score runs, the object of the fielding side is to allow as few runs as possible to be scored against them. It is much the same at Contract Bridge. The object of the Declaring Side is to score Points, the object of the Defending Side is to allow as few Points as possible to be scored against them. There is, however, one great difference—the fielding side at Cricket can never score runs, but the Defending Side at Bridge can score Points.

Having established that the object of Bridge is to score Points, let us see what these Points are and how they are scored. If you study the Table on the opposite page in the light of explanations that follow, you should be able to grasp the whole principle on which the scoring is based.

Trick Points

These are won *only* by the Declaring Side, and *only* when the Contract is fulfilled.

These Points and no others score below the line, that is count towards the Game.

Premium Points

These are divided into three classes—Penalty, Bonus and Honour. Penalty Points are won only by the Defending Side, and only when the Contract is defeated.

Bonus points are won only by the Declaring Side through:

1. Overtricks.
2. Fulfilment of doubled or redoubled Contract.
3. Slams.
4. The Rubber.

Honour Points

These are scored usually by the Declaring Side, more rarely by the Defending Side. They are the result neither of good bidding nor of good play. They depend upon the fortuitous distribution of the cards in the Deal. They have been given up mostly in Duplicate Tournaments, and their excision from Rubber Bridge is overdue.

Let us now clarify the situation by examples. Under TRICK POINTS you see that GAME is made up of 100 Trick Points. These can be won by bidding and making

1. Three No Trumps $40 + 30 + 30 = 100$.
2. Four Spades or Hearts $4 \times 30 = 120$.
3. Five Diamonds or Clubs $5 \times 20 = 100$.
4. Two spades Doubled $2 \times 60 = 120$.
5. One No Trump Redoubled $1 \times 160 = 160$.

And so on.

Remember that what you write down below the line when you fulfil your Contract is the number of Tricks mentioned in your bid multiplied by the Trick value. For example, you bid Three Spades and make four. You write 90 below the line (3×30) and 30 above (one Overtrick). Again you bid One Club, it is doubled and redoubled, and you make eight Tricks. You write 80 below the line (1×80) and 200 above (or 400 if vulnerable) for one Overtrick.

You do not have to score these 100 Points in one Contract. You can have two or more bites at the cherry, provided that the opponents do not score 100 first, for a side making Game deprives its opponents of any part-score that they may have. For example, you have 60 below the line and your opponents have 40, in the first game. If you bid and make Two Clubs this 40 Points gives you Game, and the second game is started at Love all. Your opponents can no longer use their 40 Points towards Game, though they get the credit for it in the final addition.

Under PREMIUM POINTS you will see that a side that has scored Game is said to be vulnerable. Conversely, a side that has not scored Game is said to be non-vulnerable. These clumsy terms still persist, because no one has thought of anything better. When you are vulnerable the penalties and some of the rewards are increased—that is all there is to it.

Now let us take an imaginary Rubber lasting six hands, and see how to record it on the scoring pad. Suppose that you and I cut together and that you deal the first hand. We secure the Contract with a bid of Three Hearts—you play the hand and make eleven Tricks. You and I write on our scoring pads 90 below and 60 above thus.

Note that the black line across the middle divides Trick Points from Premium Points. The first scores should be near the line, the Trick Points working downwards, the Premium Points upwards.

60	
90	

On the second hand our opponents bid One No Trump and make one Overtrick.

Now we enter the score that "they" have made, and this is how our score pads should read now. Both sides have a part-score towards the Game.

60	30
90	40

On the third hand there is a struggle for the Contract. Our opponents bid up to Three Hearts but we outbid them with Three Spades and we have no difficulty in making ten Tricks. I played the hand and as I held Ace, Queen, Knave and Ten of trumps in my own hand I get 100 Honour Points. The score now reads:

100	
30	
60	30
90	
90	40

We draw a line under this as we have made Game and our opponents lose their part-score.

We are now vulnerable and the fourth hand is dealt. Our opponents bid Four Hearts but we decide to bid Four Spades to save the Game. We are doubled and only make eight Tricks. This means that our opponents score 500 Penalty Points. So we enter this and here is the present position:

100	
30	500
60	30
90	
90	40

100		
30	500	
60	30	

The fifth hand is played by the opponents in a Contract of Three Diamonds
which they just make. This gives them
another part-score which counts towards this second Game. Here is the
score:

90		
90	40	
	60	

In the sixth and last hand we bid Four
Hearts. Our left-hand opponent doubles
but we manage to make ten Tricks. At
this stage we have not only to enter the
score for the current hand, but also to
add up and see what the result of the
Rubber is. After we have written 240
below and 50 above for Fulfilment of
Doubled Contract and 700 for Rubber
where opponents have won no Game,
we add up both sides and subtract the
opposing score from our own. The
answer is 730. That means that we have
won 700 Points.

700	
50	
100	
30	500
60	30
90	
90	40
240	60
1360	630
630	
730	

2
VALUING THE HAND

IT is essential at the outset to understand the principle that underlies bidding. Every hand dealt "belongs" to one side or the other, the disparity being sometimes small, sometimes great. When one side has an overwhelming advantage in high cards or distribution, this results in uncontested hands, where one side is left to bid with little or no interference from the opponents. When the cards are more evenly distributed, this results in competitive hands with a spirited auction, as each side attempts to reach a contract that will gain them the maximum, or *lose them the minimum*, number of points.

A partnership, therefore, must find out as quickly as possible, whether the hand belongs to them or to their opponents, and in either case they must have some method of hand valuation, so that the trick-taking capacity of their cards, whether in attack or in defence, can be assessed. Such assessment will restrict overbidding in uncontested hands and avoid loss on good cards. It will also prevent a partnership from paying too much in Penalty Points when outbidding the opponents, or from being content with too small a penalty from the opponents when they indulge in sacrifice bidding.

Before we go any further, it must be stressed that each hand of 13 cards has two values, one defensive, one attacking. In defence, that is, when the opponents are playing the hand, we rely only on first- and second-round winners, on Aces and Kings. When we are playing the hand, however, we can count on the low cards of our long suits. Consider this hand:

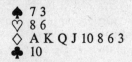

♠ 7 3
♡ 8 6
◇ A K Q J 10 8 6 3
♣ 10

This is a very simple hand to value. At a diamond contract the solidity of the diamond suit ensures the taking of eight

tricks. These eight tricks are called Playing Tricks. A little
reflection will show you that the maximum number of tricks
you can take in defence against an opposing contract in
spades, hearts, or clubs, is two, and if one of the opponents
has a singleton or void, you will take one or none.

Here you may ask, Why bother about defensive tricks?
The answer is that at the start of a hand you do not know
whether you or your opponents are going to play the hand.
If your bid did not guarantee any defensive tricks, your side
would have no means of knowing when the opponents had
bid for a contract they could not fulfil.

Since Contract Bridge appeared on the scene in the late
1920s there have been various methods of hand valuation:
Honour Tricks, Playing Tricks, and the Point Count.
Culbertson based his system on Honour Tricks, that is,
defensive tricks, while Milton Work evolved the Point Count
table, which rates an Ace as 4, a King as 3, a Queen as 2, and
a Knave as 1. This last method has to-day almost entirely
superseded Honour Tricks. For no-trump bidding on
balanced hands it is extremely accurate, but in suit bidding
on unbalanced hands no player will achieve good results by
blind faith in points alone.

Let us take a hand and consider it from three different
standpoints:

	Defensive Tricks	Point Count	Playing Tricks
♠ K Q 4	1	5	1
♡ A K 10 7 5	2	7	4
◇ Q J 10	0	3	1
♣ A Q	1	6	1

From what has already been said you will understand the
figures in the first two columns, but you might like the third
one clarified. With hearts as trumps we count two Playing
Tricks for the Ace and King, and two for the long cards.
Until we know more about the lie of the cards we assume a
normal 3–3–2 distribution of the heart suit and "give" the
Queen to the opponents. This is a rough guide as we feel our
way. We are conservative in counting only one Playing
Trick in spades and clubs, for it is clear that we shall make

two spades if the Ace is not on our left, and two tricks in clubs also, if the King is favourably placed.

Consideration of the following hands may open your eyes to the fact that distribution as well as honour strength plays a vital part in valuation:

♠ A K 2		♠ A K 5 4 3 2
♡ A K 3 2	and	♡ A K 5 4 3 2
◇ A K 2		◇
♣ A K 2		♣ 2

The first hand has a Point Count rating of 28, and with 8 Honour Tricks is in the Grand Slam Zone, according to Culbertson. Yet a beginner can see that even a nine-trick contract in no-trumps might be in jeopardy, if partner has a balanced Yarborough. The second hand has only 4 Honour Tricks, with the expectation of only seven Playing Tricks, and the Point Count rating of 14 is little more than a minimum. Common sense, however, tells us that if the partner has nothing more than four cards in spades or hearts ten tricks will be taken at the right major suit contract. And common sense is confirmed by Playing Tricks, which assess each suit at 5, giving a total of 10.

Trick-Taking Expectancy

It may be as well to point out here that Bridge is a partnership game, and that it is the best contract on 26 cards, not on 13, that is sought. Both partners must be alert to the trick-taking expectancy of the combined hands. The opening bidder by his bid guarantees a certain minimum point count or honour strength, and the responder does the same. It is the amount over and above the promised minimum that determines the later course of the bidding, as we shall see in another chapter.

The purpose of bidding in uncontested hands is to determine by intelligent communication two things, correct location and correct height. The correct location is where to play the contract, whether in spades, hearts, diamonds, clubs, or no-trumps. The correct height is at what level to play the contract, whether part score, Game, or slam.

3

OPENING NO TRUMP BIDS AND RESPONSES

W^E will start with No Trump bidding and give you a chance to see the simple operation of the Point Count, which is, as I have said, so accurate for balanced hands. Let us set out the table once more:

Ace 4   King 3   Queen 2   Knave 1

Some players count a ten as a $\frac{1}{2}$, but this is not recommended here.

Systems differ in their treatment of No Trump bidding. Some employ a variable No Trump, that is, strong when vulnerable, weak when not vulnerable, while others recommend weak throughout. Furthermore, the low limit is either 12–14 or 13–15, and the upper limit is either 15–17 or 16–18. But the system which is recommended in this book is strong throughout with 16–18 as the range.

The bid of 1 No Trump is a most valuable bid because, unlike the opening bid of one in a suit, it is limited. It announces a balanced distribution and a narrowly defined point count, so enabling the partner to assess immediately the prospects of the 26 cards of the partnership.

To qualify as an opening No Trump your hand must pass two other tests. It must have the right shape or pattern, and it must be adequately protected. The hand patterns that are permissible are three, 4–3–3–3, 4–4–3–2, and 5–3–3–2. The third of these is less common and, when used, the five-card suit should be a minor. As regards protection three suits must be fully guarded. It is, of course, desirable to have all four suits stopped, but this is a refinement that you cannot always afford, and you are allowed to have one suit unguarded. But the unguarded suit should not consist of fewer than three cards. A losing doubleton is to be deprecated.

Let us take a look at some typical hands that may be opened with 1 No Trump:

1. ♠ K 9 4   2. ♠ A K 2   3. ♠ Q 6 5
  ♡ A 10 7   ♡ A 4   ♡ K 7 6
  ◇ A J 5   ◇ A J 10 3   ◇ A K Q 7 2
  ♣ K J 6 5   ♣ Q 9 8 5   ♣ K 5

The first hand has 16 points with 3–3–3–4 shape; the second hand has 18 points with a 3–2–4–4 shape; the third hand has 17 points with 3–3–5–2 shape.

To open with a bid of Two No Trump the hand pattern is unchanged, but now all four suits should be guarded, and the Point Count is increased, the range being 20–22. The lower limit of 20 needs the additional aid of a five-card suit or good "fillers," in the shape of tens, nines, and eights. Here is an opening Two No Trump:

♠ K Q 6
♡ K J 8 5
◇ A Q 10
♣ A Q 2

It is possible to open with a bid of Three No Trump on a hand containing 25–27 points, but this is rarely done to-day, most players reserving this as a tactical bid on a hand containing a six- or seven-card solid minor suit with guards in at least two of the other suits. The general practice is to open hands as strong as this with a conventional Two Club bid (see chapter 7).

The alert reader will have noticed that no provision has been made for hands with 19, 23, or 24 points. The 19 point hand is too good for 1 No Trump and not good enough for 2 No Trump, and must be opened with a suit bid of one. The 23 and 24 point hands are opened with a conventional Two Club bid (see chapter 7).

Responding to Opening No Trump with a Balanced Hand

A No Trump response to an opening No Trump is one of the easiest things for the beginner to master. He has only to keep three numbers in mind—26, 33, and 37.

26 is the number of points required by the partnership for Game.

33 is the number of points required by the partnership for Small Slam.

37 is the number of points required by the partnership for Grand Slam.

It is, of course, possible to make nine tricks with fewer than 26 points, when the cards are favourably located, and on the other side of the ledger it is sometimes not possible to get home with 29, if the breaks are wrong or the guards inadequate, but the above table is a good guide. Here, then, are some rules.

1. With fewer than 8 points you pass, since the combined total must fall short of 26. There is, however, one exception. With 7 points and a five-card suit *that can be developed* you raise to 2 No Trump. The proviso in italics is most important —Q 10 x x x is all right, but 9 x x x x is almost worthless.

2. With 8–9 points you raise to 2 No Trump.
3. With 10–14 points you raise to 3 No Trump.
4. With 15–16 points you raise to 4 No Trump.
5. With 17–20 points you raise to 6 No Trump.
6. With more than 20 points you raise to 7 No Trump.

If you look at the second rule, you will see that as 8 or 9 points are not enough for Game, if your partner is minimum, you make a tentative suggestion by bidding 2 No Trump. This asks partner to bid Game if he has more than a minimum. Rule 4 advises another tentative bid of 4 No Trump, for you are again in the borderline zone, but on this occasion it is Slam not Game that is in doubt. Your bid asks your partner to bid 6 No Trump with more than a minimum. An experienced pair would treat 19 and 20 point hands specially, but this is beyond the scope of this book.

If your partner opens with a bid of 2 No Trump, the same key numbers will show you what action to take.

1. With 0–3 points you pass.
2. With 4–10 points you raise to 3 No Trump.
3. With 11 points you raise to 4 No Trump.
4. With 12–15 points you raise to 6 No Trump.
5. With 16–18 points you raise to 7 No Trump.

Responding to Opening No Trump with a Suit Bid

There are only three classes of suit take-outs, at the Two level, Three level, or Four level. A Five level take-out in a minor suit is not considered because of its infrequency, but it could occur on a really freak hand.

a. A Take-out at the Two level shows from 0–7 points. This is a weak bid and does not expect any further bid from the opener. The hand should be unbalanced and probably contain a singleton. For example bid 2 spades on

```
♠ 10 8 7 5 4 2
♡ 7 4
◇ K 8 5 3
♣ 9
```

Do not, however, bid 2 spades on the following hand:

```
♠ Q 9 7 4 2
♡ 9 7 3
◇ Q 9 5
♣ 6 4
```

Many poor players would bid 2 spades because "they play the weak take-out". But the Weak Take-out means that a bid of two in a suit denotes a weak hand, not that a weak hand must employ the take-out. It is better to let your partner try to make seven tricks than for you to undertake eight.

b. A Take-out at the Three level shows 8 points and over. It is unlimited, because it may range from a distributional try for Game in one of the major suits, to a full forcing bid with a slam in view. You must appreciate that this bid may be proper in a major suit, but quite wrong in a minor. Consider these two hands:

```
1. ♠ 7                    2. ♠ 7
   ♡ K Q 10 7 5             ♡ 8 5 2
   ◇ 8 5 2                  ◇ K Q 10 7 5
   ♣ A 7 6 3               ♣ A 7 6 3
```

On 1. the bid of 3 hearts is in order, as 4 hearts is a sound alternative to 3 No Trump, but on 2. the correct bid is 3 No Trump, as 5 diamonds can hardly succeed.

   c. A Take-out at the Four level shows a seven-card major suit. The points will vary from 5, if contained in the suit, to 7, if outside it.

The Stayman Convention

   No discussion of No Trump bidding can be complete without reference to the Stayman convention. The main purpose of this is to discover a 4–4 fit in a major suit, for on occasions Game can be made in the suit call when a No Trump contract would fail. The mechanics of Stayman are simple. The responder bids 2 clubs, which is a command to the opener to bid a four-card major, if he has one. With no four-card major the opener bids 2 diamonds, with one four-card major he bids two in the suit, and with four cards in both majors he bids spades first, and can bid hearts later, if the subsequent bidding seems to justify such a course. There are several variations of the convention, but the one that has been outlined is the simplest to follow.

   Stayman can also be used over an opening 2 No Trump, the response being 3 clubs, but the procedure is a little different. The opener is expected to bid his four-card suits in ascending order to discover *any* 4–4 fit, for now it is not Game, but slam possibilities that are being investigated. If the opener's only four card suit is clubs, he rebids 3 No Trump.

4

SUIT BIDS

IF you have appreciated the smooth operation of the point count in no-trump bidding, you will be anxious to know whether it can be applied to suit bidding. Indeed it can, but for the correct assessment of unbalanced hands some distributional allowance must be made. If we do not make such an allowance, we shall arrive at the ridiculous conclusion that the two hands that follow are of equal value:

♠ A Q J 9 6	♠ A Q J 9
♡ K Q J 7 5	♡ K Q J
◇ 6 4	◇ 7 6 4
♣ 8	♣ 8 6 5

Both hands have the same number of defensive tricks, both hands have the same point count, but it is clear that the first hand has greater offensive power than the second. It is the number of establishable long-card tricks that accounts for the difference. The spades and hearts in the first hand are each worth four playing tricks, two in high cards and two in low cards, giving a total trick-taking value of eight. In the second hand, however, the barren 4–3–3–3 distribution admits of only one possible long-card trick—in the spade suit—for a total of five.

How is this distributional allowance to be made? Are we to give an assessment in points to suits that consist of five or more cards? This is what the Culbertson point count system does in practice, and what other systems do in effect, though it has been found more convenient to calculate this allowance from the short suit remainders, that is, doubletons, singletons, and voids. The following table has been generally accepted:

Doubletons	1 point
Singletons	2 points
Voids	3 points

This is, undeniably, not a precise valuation, but it is good enough for our immediate purpose, which is to show you when you should open the bidding.

Though, as you have seen, 16–18 points in high cards are required for an opening 1 NT, a suit bid of one can be made with fewer points, the acceptable minimum being 12. Here, then, is the first rule for an opening bid of one in a suit:

1. A minimum point count of 12.

There are three other rules that must be complied with:

2. Two defensive tricks.
3. A biddable suit.
4. An undertaking to bid again, if partner makes a response (other than no-trumps or a raise of your suit), which is passed by the next player.

We have already discussed the first two rules, but we must go more fully into the last two.

A biddable suit is any suit of five cards or more, or any four-card suit headed by Ace, King, or Queen Knave. There is a general tendency to-day to open weaker four-card suits, but you should avoid this. To open the bidding with 1 spade on ♠ J x x x is likely to cause disaster.

The final rule, a guaranteed rebid, is vital. Without it the smooth progress of approach bidding is impossible. Furthermore, as you will see later, it determines not only what bid you should make, but whether you should or should not open the bidding.

The minimum point count has been fixed at 12, but there must also be an upper limit, and you will find 20 to be satisfactory. But you must not let yourself be bound hand and foot by these figures, for there are hands with as many as 13 points that should be passed, and some with more than 20 that should still be opened with a bid of one. Here are a few examples:

♠ A K 10 8 5 3	♠ A 8 4 3	♠ A K 8 7
♡ 7 5	♡ 9 2	♡ 4
◇ K 8 6	◇ A 8 7	◇ A K 9 5
♣ 10 4	♣ A 6 5 3	♣ A J 7 6

The first hand has a total of 12 points with a good rebiddable spade suit, and it qualifies as an opening bid of 1 spade. The second hand has 13 points, and is by some authorities regarded as an obligatory opening, but you are advised to pass with such a hand as dealer. The third hand is rated at 21 points, but not one of its three suits is strong enough to offer a play for game, unless partner can respond to a one bid.

As a general principle it is good to get your blow in first, but this principle, certainly at Duplicate, is carried too far to-day, and some of the opening bids have to be seen to be believed. You are advised, at least until you have acquired confidence through experience, to make sound opening bids. When the opening bid and the partner's response are based on solid values, there is little fear that the partners will bid themselves into some ruinous contract.

There are some hands, too strong to pass, which lack the point count for an opening 1 NT but have no biddable suit. What is to be done? Suppose you hold:

$$\spadesuit \ 9\ 7\ 6\ 5$$
$$\heartsuit \ A\ Q\ J$$
$$\diamondsuit \ K\ 8\ 4$$
$$\clubsuit \ A\ 7\ 5$$

You cannot open with 1 spade, because you know that to bid a suit as weak as x x x x especially a major, is madness, so you manufacture a bid, and open 1 club on a three-card suit. Now let me make it quite clear to you that no good player ever wants to make such a bid, but he does it in preference to passing a hand with as many as 14 high card points. Some poor players think this is a wonderful method, and they say, when you cut with them, "Do you play the Prepared Club?". Your answer should be, "Not if I can help it." You can vary your tone to suit the partner!

So far we have discussed hands containing only one biddable suit, but you will often hold two, and sometimes even three biddable suits. You must be able to decide which suit to bid first, so here are a few rules to help you.

Bidding hands with more than one biddable suit

1. With two biddable suits of equal length bid the higher

ranking first. This allows your partner, if he prefers your
first suit, to show his preference without increasing the
contract.

```
♠ A K J 9 7          ♠ A K J 9
♡ A Q 8 5 3          ♡ A Q 8 5
◇ 9 5                ◇ 9 5
♣ 4                  ♣ 7 4 3
```

In both the hands above open with 1 spade, and rebid 2
hearts over partner's 2 club response.

2. With two biddable suits of unequal length bid the
longer first.

```
♠ A K Q 9
♡ A Q J 5 3
◇ 9 5
♣ 4 3
```

Open 1 heart and rebid 2 spades over any response from
partner. But this is the moment to sound a note of warning.
You must not rebid in a shorter suit of higher rank, unless
the overall strength of your hand warrants it, because your
partner, if he prefers your first suit, will have to increase the
contract, when he shows preference. It is not easy to fix an
exact figure for a *reverse* as it is called, but approximately 18
points is desirable. The hand above, for example, has 16 high
card and 2 distributional points.

N.B. There is no reverse at the one level. If you open with
a diamond, and partner responds 1 heart, your rebid of 1
spade does *not* constitute a reverse.

It is to the genius of Culbertson that we owe the Principle
of Preparedness. You must keep this principle in mind before
you make your opening bid, and so be prepared to deal with
any possible response from partner. This is why when we
hold a hand of little more than minimum strength with
biddable suits of equal length in spades and clubs we
disregard rule 1 above, and bid 1 club on each of the hands
below:

```
♠ A K 9 7            ♠ A K 9 7 4
♡ 9 5 4              ♡ 9 5
◇ 6 3                ◇ 6
♣ A K 10 8           ♣ A K 10 8 3
```

In neither case are we strong enough to open with 1 spade and make a *high reverse* by bidding 3 clubs over a response at the two level in a red suit. But, if we replace one of the small spades with the Queen, the hands are strong enough to be bid in ranking order.

If you hold a 4–4–4–1 pattern, with three biddable suits, the recommended practice is to make your bid in the suit immediately below the singleton. Let us take two examples:

♠ A Q 10 4	♠ A Q 10 4
♡ K J 9 6	♡ K J 9 6
◇ 4	◇ K Q 6 5
♣ K Q 6 5	♣ 4

On the first hand you open with 1 club and, if partner says 1 diamond, you have a comfortable rebid of 1 spade, and can later show your hearts. On the second hand you open with 1 spade, because the spade suit is below clubs on the second time round, as it were.

5

RESPONSES TO ONE OF A SUIT

WHILE you are still in the Kindergarten you must see that your opening bids and responses are perfectly sound. Shaded bids, that is, bids made on hands which just fail to satisfy the normal requirements, may be made by experts whose skill in the play of the cards entitles them to take risks but these bids are not safe for novices. The only sound rule for the beginner is to be sure that he has the full strength which is required for the bid which he makes. If his partner is an expert he can do any shading which may be called for, and the knowledge that he can rely on the soundness of the novice's bid will be invaluable to him.

The beginner at bridge should learn thoroughly the requirements for the various responses he should make to his partner's opening bid. All that he knows when he has to consider his first response is that his partner has a hand which is better than the average and that he has a biddable suit. The opening bid may have been made on a hand containing only the minimum strength required, but it is possible that it may have been made on a hand so strong that it requires little help from him to make game. It is his duty if possible to make some bid which will give his partner a chance to bid again and in making his response he has to consider how he can best indicate to the opener the character of his own hand.

In the early days of Contract, with the vast range of the one-bid in the Culbertson system, the responder felt obliged to keep the bidding open on the proverbial shoestring. Expert practice to-day is more conservative, and a response is not given without 6, or on occasions 5, points.

There are four things that you can do as responder, when your partner opens the bidding with one in a suit:

1. Pass.
2. Raise your partner's suit.

3. Bid No Trumps.

4. Take out in a suit of your own.

It will be helpful to discuss these four different courses of action:

1. The Pass, which has no subdivisions, shows from 0–5 points. For example, the opener has bid 1 heart, and you pass with

♠ Q 7 5
♥ 9 5 2
♦ Q J 6 3
♣ 8 6 4

2. The Raise of your partner's suit. Before you proceed any further you must realise that, as responding hand in support of your partner's suit, you have to revise the values of your voids and singletons. The short suit remainders are no longer merely an indirect assessment of your own hand pattern with no intrinsic trick-taking value, but now, in support of your partner's suit, they can furnish tricks just like Aces and Kings, as long as you have sufficient trumps. Therefore the void is rated at 5 instead of 3, and the single-ton at 3 instead of 2. With these new figures in mind we can study the subdivisions of the raise.

a. The Single Raise shows from 6–9 points. The opener bids 1 heart and you raise to 2 hearts with either of the hands below:

♠ 7 4   ♠ 9 7 5
♥ Q 8 6 5   ♥ K 8 5 4
♦ Q J 7 6   ♦ A 8 2
♣ 8 7 2   ♣ Q 6 4

The first hand is a minimum. The second hand is a maximum in high cards, but you see that the fourth trump is virtually worthless because of the barren distribution.

b. The Double Raise shows from 10–12 points. You raise your partner's 1 heart to 3 hearts with

♠ 8 7
♥ K 10 7 3
♦ A 10 6 4
♣ K J 2

A double raise guarantees at least four trumps.

c. The Treble Raise shows from 13–15 points. Suppose you hold the hands below after an opening 1 heart by partner:

♠ 6	♠ K 7 4
♡ K 9 7 6 5	♡ K 9 7 6 5
◇ A Q J	◇ A 9 8 6 4
♣ 9 6 4 3	♣

The first hand has 13 points and is a good raise to 4 hearts. The hand has no great defence against an opposing spade contract, and the jump to game may serve to keep the opponents from getting together. As a matter of fact, there is to-day a tendency to make this bid on weaker hands, as a pure shut out bid. The second hand is theoretically a maximum, but with its two first- and two second-round controls it is really far stronger than the point count makes it. No expert player would raise to 4 hearts on it, but would sound out the slam possibilities, either by making a forcing bid of 3 diamonds, or by making a delayed game raise, by bidding 2 diamonds, followed by a raise to 4 hearts, indicating a hand too good for a mere raise to game.

The treble raise unconditionally promises four trumps, with a strong suggestion of five. The fifteen points will be divided between high cards and distribution in the ratio of 10 to 5 approximately. This is obvious, because with 15 points in high cards the shape would be balanced, and some different bid should be sought.

You will have noticed that the raises discussed have been confined to an opening bid in a major suit. There is a reason for this. The ruffing factor that is present in a suit contract can provide one extra trick, and so offset the disadvantage of the ten-trick major suit contract as compared with No Trumps, but it cannot so readily produce the *two* extra tricks needed for game in a minor suit. So, when your partner opens the bidding with one in a minor, even if you have good support, you are always on the look out for an easier road to game. If your hand warrants a treble raise, you give only a double raise, so that you do not cut out the shortest route to game in 3 NT. Of course, with a really freak hand, or when other factors show that a No Trump contract is undesirable, you decide to go for the eleven-trick contract.

We have covered the raises of a major suit opening, but there is the rare raise to game in a minor suit to be considered. This indicates a freak distribution, something like 1–1–6–5. Five trumps are guaranteed, and quite possibly six. While writing this paragraph I received a query from someone, asking me what to bid on this hand:

♠ A
♡ J
♢ Q 10 9 8 5 4
♣ Q 10 6 4 3

This is a raise to 5 diamonds. Such a raise is mostly preemptive and does not imply a wealth of high cards.

3. No Trump responses. Remember that there is no distributional allowance for any No Trump responses. They are made on balanced hands and are limit bids.

a. A response of 1 NT shows 6–9 points. If partner opens with 1 spade you bid 1 NT on the following:

♠ 10 6	♠ 10 6
♡ K 7 5 3	♡ A 7 5 3
♢ K 7 4	♢ K 7 4
♣ 10 8 6 2	♣ Q 8 6 2

b. A response of 2 NT shows 11–12 points. This bid is grossly abused especially by brash players who do not understand its finer points. Take these hands:

♠ A 8 7	♠ A 8 7 5
♡ Q 4	♡ K J 3
♢ Q 10 7 6	♢ Q 8 2
♣ K 5 4	♣ Q 6 5

The first hand with only 11 points is an excellent response of 2 NT to 1 heart, with support, but not *too much*, in hearts and a well guarded Queen in diamonds. The second hand with 12 points is a bad 2 NT response. There is too much in hearts, and the minor suit Queens are very poorly protected. The correct response is 1 spade.

c. A response of 3 NT shows 13–15 points. This response too is abused, especially by those players who want to play the hand. I make the lower limit of this response 13 because this is popular practice, but except for psychological reasons I myself never jump *immediately* to 3 NT on a bare 13 points, but look for some other bid first. The hand that follows is a good 3 NT response to an opening 1 heart:

♠ A J 5
♡ K 7
♢ K Q 8 4
♣ Q 9 8 6

4. Responses in a New Suit. These again fall into three classes:

a. One over One, that is, a response in a higher ranking suit at the same level.

b. Take out at the Two-level, that is, a response in a lower ranking suit.

c. Forcing take out, at the Two level in a higher ranking suit, or at the Three level in a lower ranking suit.

Let us take these three classes in order.

a. A one over one response is an unlimited bid showing 6–15 points. For example, over an opening 1 heart you respond 1 spade on either of these hands:

♠ K J 10 6 5   ♠ A J 10 7 5
♡ 7 4 2   ♡ K J 2
♢ Q 9 4   ♢ K 10 4
♣ 10 8   ♣ Q 2

The first hand is little better than a minimum and keeps the bidding open with the suggestion of an alternative contract in spades. The second hand is a typical one over one response, not quite good enough for a forcing take out, but ready to bid for game, as soon as the opener's rebid has made clear *where* the hand is to be played. If he gives a single raise in spades you bid 4 spades, if he bids 2 hearts or 2 diamonds you bid 4 hearts, and if he bids 2 clubs you jump to 3 NT.

   b. A take out at the Two level shows 9–15 points. For example, over an opening 1 heart you respond 2 clubs on the following:

♠ 10 7 5	♠ 9 7	♠ 9 7
♡ 9 6	♡ K 10 7 2	♡ K 10 7 2
♢ K 8 4	♢ 6 5	♢ A 5
♣ A Q 10 7 6	♣ K Q 10 7 6	♣ K Q 10 7 6

The first hand, a minimum, teaches no special lesson, but the other two should be studied carefully. The second hand is a frequently occurring type on which you would like to raise your partner to 2½ hearts, and you can show this by following your 2 club take out with a heart raise. The third hand is too good for an immediate raise to game and not quite good enough for a forcing take out, and you can show this by following your 2 club take out with a raise to 4 hearts. This is the Delayed Game Raise referred to on page 40.

   c. A forcing take out shows 16 points and over. This bid is forcing to game. Neither partner may pass until a game contract is reached, or the opponents have been doubled in a sacrificial bid that seems certain to bring in adequate compensation in penalty points.

   Critics have tried to make out that the forcing bid loses a round of bidding, but this is not so. The knowledge that the partnership is committed to game allows each partner to proceed quietly, without the wild leaps occasioned by the fear of being left short of game.

   When Contract was in its infancy it was widely held that a forcing take out should only be made with a fit in the opener's suit. This, of course, is an absurd platform on which to stand. The fit with the opener's suit will generally be there, but it is by no means essential, if the responder has a solid suit of his own. The real need is for the responder to have a clear idea of where the hand is to be played. Consider these two hands:

♠ K J 2	♠ K 6 3
♡ A Q 10 4	♡ 6
♢ 9 4	♢ A 4
♣ A Q J 3	♣ A K Q J 10 7 3

A forcing bid of 3 clubs over 1 heart is correct in each case. In the first hand the responder has made up his mind that hearts is to be the final contract, and the forcing bid will allow the slam possibilities to be quietly explored. In the second hand the responder, with a self-supporting suit of his own, is not concerned about having a singleton in his partner's suit. He has made up his mind to play in clubs (or possibly in No Trumps), and is primarily interested in the number of Aces that the opener holds.

6
REBIDS

THE opening bid of one in a suit, and the response to it, as we have seen in the previous chapters, are necessarily tentative. The opening bid is tentative because the strength or weakness of the partner is at first quite unknown, and the response is tentative because the opener's upper limit and his hand pattern are not yet revealed. But on the second round, in the light of what has so far been discovered both partners are in a position to show their full potential.

It is necessary to treat the opener's rebid in detail, as it is accuracy in this department that leads to successful partnership bidding. Though we are primarily concerned in this chapter with suit rebids, we will first briefly discuss the rebids of the 1 NT opener.

Do not forget the key numbers 26, 33, and 37 already mentioned.

a. If 1 NT is raised to 3 NT or 6 NT, the opener passes. As he has already limited his hand by his opening bid he cannot "find" more points and bid again.

b. If 1 NT is raised to 2 NT the opener passes with 16, bids 3 NT with 18, and should almost always bid game with 17, unless there is some weakness. This may be an unguarded suit or *lack of Aces*. I italicise this weakness because it is a serious one. Aceless wonders with a minimum point count usually fail to bring home the nine tricks.

c. If 1 NT is raised to 4 NT, you are advised to bid 6 NT only with a maximum of 18, at least until you have become a reasonable dummy player.

If the response to 1 NT is two in a suit this bid should be passed nine times out of ten. If the response is 2 clubs (not Stayman) or 2 diamonds, it is suggested that a raise be given only with a fully protected maximum and the holding of A K x or A Q x in the suit. This asks partner to bid 3 NT,

if he holds six cards to the King or Queen and some slight
extra value. Consider this hand:

♠ K 6 5	♠ Q 8 7
♡ Q J 9	♡ 6 2
◇ A Q 6	◇ K 10 7 5 3 2
♣ A Q 9 5	♣ 7 5

West opens 1 NT and East responds 2 diamonds. West with
18 points and no suit unguarded bids 3 diamonds and East,
with six diamonds to the King and the Queen of spades,
obeys orders and bids 3 NT. If the response is two in a major
a raise to three should be given only with a maximum and
exceptional support for the suit.

If the response to 1 NT is three in a major the opener
should rebid 3 NT only with a doubleton in the suit. Otherwise give a raise, or accept the suit by cue bidding an Ace.

If the response is three in a minor rebid 3 NT only with a
doubleton in the suit. Otherwise raise the suit or cue bid an
Ace. If the responder knows what he is doing his bid is not
an indirect and lazy way of saying 3 NT, but an attempt to
reach a slam.

Rebid after opening one in a suit

1. After a response of 1 NT.

We will assume in all cases that the opener has bid 1 heart.
Keep clearly in mind that after a 1 NT response, unlike a one
over one, a rebid by the opener is not mandatory. High
cards and shape will determine what rebid, if any, is called
for.

a. A pass shows a balanced hand with minimum values.

b. A rebid of 2 hearts shows little more than a minimum,
but prefers the suit contract. Consider the hands below:

♠ 9 4 3	♠ 9 4
♡ A K Q 9 5	♡ A J 9 8 6 3
◇ 8 6	◇ K 5
♣ K Q 7	♣ A 7 2

With the first hand a pass is unquestionably correct, for the heart suit may provide five tricks, but poor players will bid 2 hearts without a second thought. With the second hand a rebid of 2 hearts is in order, because the suit contract must be safer.

c. A raise to 2 NT shows 17 to 18 balanced points, and a raise to 3 NT shows 19 to 20.

d. A rebid of 3 hearts shows almost certainly a six-card suit something like 16 to 18 points, and seven playing tricks. Here is such a hand:

♠ 10 6
♡ A K J 10 8 5
◇ A 6 2
♣ K 7

e. A rebid of two in a lower ranking suit may have, but does not guarantee, extra strength. It offers a second suit and allows the responder to give preference without increasing the contract. For example:

♠ 5
♡ A Q J 8 5
◇ A K 10 6
♣ 10 8 3

You open 1 heart and over the 1 NT response rebid 2 diamonds. The responder with more diamonds than hearts passes, but with an equal number bids 2 hearts.

f. A rebid of two in a higher ranking suit is not forcing, but it must show a strong hand because preference for the first suit entails increasing the contract. The opener is, by inference, strong enough to play for nine tricks. For example:

♠ A K Q 9
♡ A Q J 5 3
◇ 9 5
♣ 4 3

g. A Jump Rebid in a new suit is forcing to game. The responder must be careful not to make a stolid rebid of

3 NT, when the opener is clearly asking for preference. Consider:

♠ A Q J 9 5	♠ 10 6
♡ A K Q 8 3	♡ J 5 4
◇ K 9	◇ A J 5 2
♣ 7	♣ Q 8 6 3

After 1 spade—1 NT West makes a forcing rebid of 3 hearts. For East to say 3 NT is very bad—he should raise to 4 hearts. With three cards in both major suits he gives spade preference, and only with a small doubleton in both can 3 NT be tolerated.

2. After a response of 2 NT. We again assume that opener has bid 1 heart. The opener is under no obligation to bid again.

a. A pass shows a balanced minimum.

b. 3 hearts shows an unbalanced minimum, with almost certainly a six-card suit, and an unwillingness to play at the game level.

c. 4 hearts shows enough values for game, some 15 to 16 points, and a six-card suit in all probability.

d. Three in another suit. This is forcing, and it asks for preference to be shown if possible.

e. 3 NT accepts the responder's invitation to play in NT, and offers from 14 to 19 balanced points.

3. After a raise. We assume that the responder raises 1 heart to 2 hearts. As responder shows from 6 to 9 points your correct procedure is:

a. Pass with 12 to 16 points.

b. 3 hearts with 17 to 19 points. Among experienced players this bid is rarely made. Instead a Trial Bid of three in a lower ranking suit may be used (with implications that vary with the partnership understanding), asking responder to take the final decision and bid game in the first suit, if the raise was based on substantial values.

c. 4 hearts with 20 points and over, or a good 19.

After a double raise you should bid game if you have anything over a minimum.

4. After a response of one in a suit. We assume that the opener says 1 heart and the responder 1 spade. You have given an undertaking to bid again, so you must find the rebid that best describes your strength and distribution. Let us take a look at some possible rebids:

a. 1 NT shows a balanced hand, with a heart suit not rebiddable, no second suit to offer, and no good support for spades.

b. 2 NT and 3 NT both show a balanced hand, the first promising 17 to 18 points, the second 19 to 20.

c. 2 spades shows trump support, preferably four cards, though sometimes the raise must be given on three to an honour, and 15 to 16 points.

d. 3 spades shows certainly four trumps, preferably to an honour, and 17 to 18 points.

e. 4 spades shows at least four trumps to an honour and 19 to 20 points.

f. Three in a lower ranking suit. This bid is known as a Jump Shift, and is forcing to game. It can be made on hands of two different types:

1. A genuine two-suiter. For example:

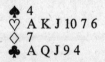

♠ 4
♡ A K J 10 7 6
♢ 7
♣ A Q J 9 4

You open 1 heart, and over 1 spade you rebid 3 clubs.

2. An exceptional fit with your partner's response. For example:

♠ K J 7 5
♡ A K J 9 6
♢ A K 2
♣ 6

You open 1 heart, and over 1 spade you rebid 3 diamonds, following with a raise to 4 spades. This rebid is most important. It paints a picture of your hand, not only showing the diamond control, but pinpointing the club singleton.

Over a response of two in a lower ranking suit the opener will rebid in much the same way as over a one over one response, but he will remember that the responder has shown a minimum of not 6 but 9 points.

Rebids by the Responder

At the responder's second opportunity to bid he has heard two bids from the opener. If the opener has given an accurate indication of his high card strength and distribution, the responder is now in a position to decide whether the partnership is to play at part score, game, or slam. The responder's rebid carries a great weight of responsibility.

It is neither practicable nor necessary to examine all possible responses, but it will be helpful to show you some actual hands, with the rebids and responses tabulated. It will be most instructive to consider the responder's rebid after a one over one response, because the first response with its range of 6 to 16 points leaves a great deal of clarification for the second response.

We assume an opening 1 heart and a 1 spade response. For example:

♠ K J 7 6 4
♡ 9 5
♢ Q 10 6
♣ 9 7 3

With this poor hand the responder is prepared to pass any rebid by the opener that is not forcing, that is, any bid except 3 diamonds and 3 clubs. Now let us look at a different type of hand:

♠ A 9 6 5 3
♡ K J 5
♢ 8
♣ K 10 7 2

With this hand, which has the values for an opening bid, the responder has already made up his mind not to stop short of game. He is only waiting for the opener's rebid to decide *where* the contract should be played. Let us tabulate some possible rebids by the opener, and the corresponding replies by the responder:

	Opener	*Responder*
1.	1 NT	3 hearts

This rebid is forcing, and offers a choice of hearts or no trumps. The responder has clearly only three hearts, for with the same strength and four hearts he would have bid 4 hearts.

2.	2 NT	3 hearts

Here again the choice of playing in hearts is given by this forcing rebid.

3.	2 hearts	4 hearts

As soon as the hearts are rebid the responder bids game in that suit.

4.	2 spades	4 spades

Spade support with the opener is all the responder needs to know.

5.	2 diamonds	4 hearts

Here the responder is too good to give even Jump Preference by bidding 3 hearts, and must bid game.

6.	3 clubs	4 clubs

After the opener's forcing Jump Shift the responder is content to give a single raise. The small slam is certain, and the quiet approach bid will allow the grand slam possibilities to be more easily investigated.

Preference Bidding

We have more than once mentioned the word *preference*. As both partners, and particularly the responder, are

frequently asked to give preference, you must be quite clear
what this means. Let us take these two minimum hands:

♠ K J 7 6 4   ♠ K J 7 6 4
♡ 9 5 3   ♡ 9 5
♢ Q 10 3   ♢ Q 10 3
♣ 9 7   ♣ 9 7 3

Your partner opens 1 heart, and you respond 1 spade. When
your partner rebids 2 clubs, which is not forcing, you are
anxious to drop the bidding, but you must not do so. You
have not completed your duty. You have been asked for
preference, whether you prefer hearts or clubs. As you prefer
hearts to clubs you show this by bidding 2 hearts. This, be it
understood, is in no sense a raise. It is equivalent to a pass,
and we call this Primary Preference.

With the second hand you prefer clubs, and you show this
by passing. This we call Passing Preference. Now let us
consider another hand:

♠ K Q 8 4
♡ K 7 3
♢ Q 5 4
♣ 7 6 2

After 1 heart you respond 1 spade. Now your partner says
2 diamonds. you give primary preference with 2 hearts, and
look to me for approval. But you don't get it! You must not
give primary preference, which is the equivalent of a pass,
for this hand is good enough for a heart raise, and you give
it by Jump Preference, by bidding 3 hearts. This is not
forcing, so you now see why in No. 5 on page 51, you were
too good, as I said, for mere jump preference.

7
TWO BIDS

IN the relatively unenlightened days of Auction Bridge, if your contract was 1 spade and you made twelve tricks, you received the game and slam bonus with no effort on your part. But when Contract took over, with the stipulation that games and slams had to be bid before they could be scored, a need was felt for an opening bid that would enable a player with a very powerful hand to insist that the bidding be kept open until a game contract was reached. This would allow more time to find out the best contract.

When Culbertson introduced his system, this need was catered for by treating a two bid in any suit as forcing to game. The so-called negative response to such a two bid, denying the values for a positive response, was 2 NT. This has the obvious disadvantage, when the final contract is 3 NT, of exposing the strong hand on the table. Not only does this make the correct line of defence far easier to see, but it means that the opening lead goes through the strength instead of up to it.

For this reason a conventional Two Club bid has been widely adopted as the only forcing-to-game bid. This is an artificial bid, guaranteeing no specific holding in the club suit. It announces a hand that contains five Quick Tricks and sufficient playing strength to make game likely, even if the partner's hand is very weak. The negative response is 2 diamonds. Now this response does not mean that the responder necessarily has a worthless hand, though this may be the case, but it denies the values for a positive response, which can be one of three things:

a. An Ace and a King.
b. Three Kings.
c. A King and a King-Queen.

It is good for beginners to stick to the rules, but I would

point out that most first class players would make a positive
response of 2 spades or 2 hearts, if they held A Q J x x in a
major suit.

At this stage you ought to study an opening Two Club bid,
and see how good bidding by the partners arrives at an
excellent contract.

♠ A K Q 8 3	♠ 7 2
♡ A K Q 7 5	♡ J 8 4 3
◇ 4	◇ 9 6 2
♣ A 7	♣ K 9 6 5

West opens the bidding with 2 clubs. This conventional bid
says: "I have five Quick Tricks, and a hand that will make
game with but little assistance."

East responds 2 diamonds, a conventional bid which says:
"I do not have the qualifications for a positive response."

West now says 2 spades, a natural bid meaning: "I have a
spade suit."

East replies 2 NT, a mark time bid which says: "I cannot
support spades, nor have I any suit of my own to show."

West says 3 hearts, a natural bid meaning: "I also have a
heart suit."

East replies 4 hearts, which says: "I can support hearts."

West now bids 5 clubs, a cue bid (of which we will learn
later). Its message is: "I have the Ace of clubs. Have you by
any chance the King?"

East says 6 clubs—"Yes, I have the King."

West bids 6 hearts, which becomes the final contract. Without this conventional bid which allows the quiet exchange of
information under the game contract guarantee, West would
have had to shut his eyes and bid game in one of his suits.

As was said earlier on page 29, the practice of most
experts to-day is to open 23 and 24 point balanced hands
with a Two Club bid, and to follow a 2 diamond response
with a 2 NT rebid. This bid may be passed by the responder
if he holds fewer than three points. Let us look at this hand:

♠ A K 9	♠ 10 7 3
♡ A Q 3	♡ 10 8 5 4
◇ A J 7	◇ Q 8 4 2
♣ K Q 8 5	♣ 7 6 3

West bids 2 clubs, East responds 2 diamonds, and West
rebids 2 NT. East with only two points passes. It must be
stressed that this sequence (2 ♣–2 ◇–2 NT) is the *only* one
that can be dropped short of game. If 2 ♣–2 ◇ is followed
by a suit rebid, this is forcing to game.

As we reserve the Two Club bid for game going hands
that contain five Quick Tricks, we can use other two bids in
spades, hearts, and diamonds to describe hands of great
distributional power, based on eight playing tricks with the
declared suit as trumps. This two bid, which is forcing for
one round, is part of the Acol system and is played by most
good players to-day. Theoretically the bid guarantees no
specific high card strength or point count, but in practice we
see that there must be some such valuation, for a hand such
as ♠ A K Q J 10 8 6 5 ♡ 4 ◇ 6 5 ♣ 8 4 does not qualify
as an opening 2 spade bid, and is opened with a preemptive
bid. On the other hand it must have fewer than five Quick
Tricks, because that type of hand is catered for by the Two
Club bid. Somewhere between these two extremes lies the
requisite high card strength, and though this is not easy to
determine exactly, let us say that $3\frac{1}{2}$–4 Quick Tricks is about
right. For example:

> ♠ A K Q 10 8 5
> ♡ 9 2
> ◇ A 7 6
> ♣ A 10

A strong two-suiter may also be opened with this two bid.
For example:

> ♠ A K 10 9 7 6
> ♡ A Q J 8 5
> ◇ 8
> ♣ 4

Responses to an opening Two Bid

1. The negative response, corresponding to 2◇ over 2♣,
is 2 NT.

2. A single raise of the opener's suit shows trump support,
such as Q x or x x x, in addition to an Ace. This bid is

unlimited, and there is no need to give more than a single raise, however strong your hand. It is vital to give this early raise in your partner's suit, if you have the qualifications, as accurate slam bidding depends on it.

3. A double raise denotes good trump support, some scattered honour strength, about 9 or 10 points, *but no Ace*.

4. In order to bid a suit of his own the responder must have a biddable suit and at least one Quick Trick, if the level is not raised. If the suit necessitates a response at the three level, an additional King should be held. For example:

<table>
<tr><td>♠ K Q 10 8 7</td><td>♠ 8 5</td></tr>
<tr><td>♡ 8 5</td><td>♡ K Q 10 8 7</td></tr>
<tr><td>◇ J 7 2</td><td>◇ J 7 2</td></tr>
<tr><td>♣ 10 6 4</td><td>♣ K 6 4</td></tr>
</table>

In the first hand a response of 2 spades over an opening 2 hearts is in order, but the second hand requires the addition of the King of clubs, to justify 3 hearts over an opening 2 spades.

5. A response of 3 NT shows 11–12 points, similar to a response of 2 NT over a one bid. It denies an Ace, and by inference denies good support for the opener's suit.

Rebids by the opening Two Bidder

Over a negative 2 NT response the opening bidder rebids three in his suit if he has a minimum of eight playing tricks. With more he jumps to game.

If the opener has a second suit he bids it. This is not forcing, though in practice it will be passed only with a very weak hand. If the two suiter is exceptionally strong, the opener must make a jump rebid in the second suit.

It is as well to point out, though many players pay scant attention to this fact, that with diamonds as your long suit you require eleven tricks for game, so that you really need an extra winner for your two bid.

8

PREEMPTIVE BIDS AND RESPONSES

OPENING bids of three and four in any suit and of five in a minor suit are preemptive bids. Their sole object is to sever the enemy lines of communication, either by preventing them from entering the bidding altogether, or by restricting their bidding space. Let us take the hand that appears on page 54:

♠ A K Q 8 3	♠ 7 2
♡ A K Q 7 5	♡ J 8 4 3
◇ 4	◇ 9 6 2
♣ A 7	♣ K 9 6 5

where we saw that, left to their own devices, EW reached a very good contract of 6 hearts after an opening bid of 2 clubs by West. But suppose that South had dealt himself this hand:

♠ 5
♡ 6 2
◇ A K Q 10 8 7 5 3
♣ 10 5

If not vulnerable against vulnerable opponents South opens with a bid of 5 diamonds, three tricks above the trick-taking capacity of his hand. Now what is West to do? If he doubles his side will score 500, which is a poor substitute for the 1630 they would have received for finishing the rubber with 6 hearts. If West bids 5 spades he will go down. If he is clairvoyant and bids 5 hearts, East will not raise to the slam.

The value of a game is on the average 500 points, and preemptive bids are based on this figure. From this was developed the Culbertson rule of Two and Three, which is preached by most players, if not always practised. This means that, if vulnerable you can overbid your hand by two tricks, if not vulnerable by three, the penalty in each case being 500, if the contract is doubled. When the opening

bidder makes a preemptive bid he is in fact saying to his
partner that, in his opinion, the enemy have the balance of
power and, if given the necessary bidding space, will bid
themselves comfortably to game or slam. There is, then, no
point count qualification for a preemptive bid—it is purely a
question of playing tricks. There are, however, two conditions that you should observe, when you decide to
preempt:

1. The hand must not be too strong. The holding of two
defensive tricks rules out a preemptive bid. (In the 5 diamond
bid illustrated above Ace and King do not count as two
defensive tricks in an *eight-card* suit.)

2. The suit must not be too weak. This second condition
is continually disregarded, especially by duplicate players,
but I am all for having a solid suit, even if that solidarity
does not start at the top. For example:

♠ Q J 10 9 7 5 4 3
♡ 8
◇ 9 4
♣ K Q

is a good bid of 3 spades, but to make this bid on the
following hand

♠ K 9 8 6 5 4 2
♡ 8
◇ 9 4
♣ A 8 5

is stupid. I would rather open with 1 spade.

I have chosen spades in each of the above examples
because a bid at the three level in spades, and to a lesser
degree in hearts, is effective in its attempt to interfere with
the enemy intelligence organisation, but three bids in minor
suits have not the same power. It is my own feeling that
minor suit preemptive bids should be at the four and five
levels. This allows us to base our minor three bids on a solid
suit such as A K Q x x x x, thus offering, in addition to the
mild preemptive offensive against the opponents, something
constructive on which our partner, who may have a very
good hand, can build.

Let us be honest in our appraisal of the preemptive bid. It is its timing that gives it force. It is not the answer to a maiden's prayer. If you deal and bid 3 spades when your partner has a huge hand, you have not been clever. If your opponents have all the high cards, your timing has been excellent. Do not forget that your partner is shut out as well as the opponents.

Countering the Preemptive Bid

Once the preemptive bid was established, there arose a need for some means to counter it. None of the methods current to-day are satisfactory, for the preempt, if *intelligently* employed, is difficult to meet. There are times when, to use the tournament player's lament, you have got to let yourself "be fixed." If you think that you are going to obtain a perfect result on every occasion, you will be sadly disillusioned. There will be many occasions when the preempt will fail in its object, but there will also be times when it will succeed. If you obstinately refuse to allow this, you will be playing right into the hands of the preempter. Play it cool, and you will find that because of the number of points that you gain from preemption made against you, you can afford to give it best now and then.

There are three main methods of defence:

1. 3 NT as a request to partner to bid his best suit. The great disadvantage of this convention is that it makes it almost impossible to play the hand in 3 NT, though this may be the only contract. Furthermore, if the preempt is in a minor suit, the bidding has been taken unnecessarily high.

2. The Lower Minor. This means that over 3 clubs you bid 3 diamonds as a take out, and 4 clubs over other three bids.

3. The Optional Double. This is what I consider the best of a bad bunch. The double is primarily for a take out, but it allows your partner to pass for penalties, if he holds the balance of the opener's suit. Its disadvantage is that, if you sit immediately over the preempter with strength in his suit, you are forced to pass.

Action of the Responder

If you are the partner of the preempter you can raise him on a good hand. Do not forget that all he has promised you is seven playing tricks, with possibly no Quick Trick, so that you will need three to four tricks, of which two must almost certainly be Aces, to raise him. You can raise 3 spades to 4 spades on this hand:

♠ 10 4
♡ A 6 3
◇ K 9 5 2
♣ A Q 8 7

You can also raise your partner on a bad hand! This is to add to the opponents' difficulties, when there is now no doubt that they have most of the cards. Take this hand:

♠ A 7 6 4 2
♡ J 10 5 4
◇ 7
♣ 10 8 3

Your partner, not vulnerable, opens with a bid of 3 spades, and the next player, who is vulnerable, bids 4 clubs for a take out. You should bid 5 spades. This may well cause the opponents to double instead of making an easy slam, or it may provoke them into bidding a slam that is not there, or to bid it in the wrong suit.

It is general practice to regard any bid over the opening preempt as encouraging, so that if you have a suit of your own, you will only be allowed to play with it as trumps, if you can make a jump bid to avoid all doubt. If your partner bids 3 hearts and you have the ten top spades, you jump to 4 spades, which should shut up even the most ardent Saint George or Joan of Arc. But if you have the ten top hearts, you will not be allowed to play in 4 hearts over an opening 3 spades!

To end this chapter let me repeat this word of advice. When you are the opponent of the preempter do not let yourself be tricked by fear, irritation, or a false sense of pride into making bids that a moment's reflection would show to be insane.

9

SLAM BIDDING

T HE slam premiums are considerable. A small slam bid and made earns a bonus of 500 points for a declarer who is not vulnerable, and 750 for one who is, while the grand slam bonus is 1000 and 1500 respectively. It is obvious, therefore, that slam bidding is a very important factor in every form of Bridge, whether rubber, team of four, or match-pointed pairs. Quite apart from the premiums, there is great satisfaction in bidding a slam, especially when it requires good play to make it.

If from laziness or diffidence you decide that slams are not for you, let me tell you that you will miss a tremendous lot of fun, you will remain a bad player, and you will be a big loser. To pay your opponents extra for their good cards without receiving for your own is bad economics.

As you may guess, in order to facilitate the bidding of slams, "they have sought out many inventions." The opening two bid, the forcing take out, and the point count itself in the early stages of bidding all play their part in the quest for slams, but there are three methods you may use for slam bidding. They are concerned primarily with locating Aces, for there is no greater ignominy than to bid a small slam and lose the first two tricks to opposing Aces. These methods are:

1. Direct Method.
2. Cue Bids.
3. Four No Trump Convention.

The first method is frequently employed for no trump slams, because with a point count based only on high cards simple arithmetic will show that two Aces cannot be missing. Suppose you hold:

♠ A 8 7
♡ K Q 7 5
♢ A Q 10 4
♣ K 6 2

Your partner bids 1 NT. His minimum 16, added to your 18, makes 34, which is enough for a small slam (see page 16). As you have all but 6 of the 40 points, you cannot be missing two Aces. You jump straight to 6 NT.

It is, of course, possible to employ the direct method in suit slams, but the distributional count may indicate twelve winners without detecting that there are two fast losers. For this reason it is safer to use one of the other methods for reaching slams in suit bids.

The second method is exploratory and is directed towards finding out if partner's values are in the right places. You have already been shown an example of cue bidding on page 54, where West's 5 club bid showed the Ace of clubs, and East's 6 clubs showed the King.

The third method is an attempt to show and locate Aces and Kings *wholesale*. There are two subdivisions of this:

1. The Culbertson Four-Five No Trump.
2. The Blackwood Four No Trump.

The first of these is incomparably the better system, but it has been passed over by a lazy-minded Bridge public in favour of the Blackwood, which is simpler. For all that we should take a brief look at this convention.

The bid of 4 NT is unconditionally forcing, and guarantees that the bidder holds *either* three Aces *or* two Aces and the King of a suit bid by the partnership. The responder's procedure is strictly defined:

1. With two Aces; *or* with one Ace
   and the Kings of *all* bid suits   5 NT

2. With one Ace or void in an un-
   bid suit   5 in that suit

3. With one Ace in a bid suit or
   the Kings of *all* bid suits   6 in the best trump

4. With no Ace he signs off in 5 of
   the lowest bid suit

Let us now take a look at the Blackwood. The 4 NT bid is

again forcing, but the bidder makes no guarantee about his own holding. The responder gives the following replies:

1. With no Ace or *with all four Aces* — 5 clubs
2. With one Ace — 5 diamonds
3. With two Aces — 5 hearts
4. With three Aces — 5 spades

If the 4 NT bidder follows with a bid of 5 NT, he is asking the responder to give information about Kings on the same scale, except that 6 clubs indicates no King, and 6 NT indicates four Kings.

It will perhaps be most helpful for you to see how the two systems operate on the same hand.

♠ A Q J 9 7	♠ K 10 5 2
♡ A Q 10 6 5	♡ K 3
◇ A 8	◇ 9 4
♣ 6	♣ A K Q 8 4

The bidding between West and East proceeds 1 spade—3 clubs—3 hearts—3 spades—4 NT. Where Culbertson is being played the responder now says 5 NT. This shows the Ace of clubs and the Kings of all the suits bid by the partnership, which makes it easy for West to bid 7 spades.

Where Blackwood is being played the responder says 5 diamonds, showing one Ace. Now if the opener asks for Kings by a 5 NT bid, he receives the reply of 5 spades, showing three Kings, but he does not know which they are. If it is the King of hearts that is missing, he does not want to bid the grand slam. However, a more intelligent West does not bid 5 NT over 5 diamonds, but makes a cue bid of 6 diamonds. This allows East to show the King of hearts by a bid of 6 hearts, and the grand slam can now be bid with confidence. You see here that Blackwood and a cue bid can and should be combined, as the occasion demands.

The beginner is strongly advised to use Blackwood as a means of avoiding an unmakeable slam, rather than as a bulldozer to push him into it. For example:

♠ 9   ♠ K Q 5
♡ A K J 7 3   ♡ Q 9 8 6 2
◇ K Q 10 4   ◇ 9 6
♣ A J 6   ♣ K 10 7

With West the opener, the bidding goes 1 heart—3 hearts—
4 NT—5 clubs—5 hearts. Though disappointed by the 5 club
response, showing no Aces, West plays without anxiety in
5 hearts.

At this point it must be stressed that you must be careful
when your trump suit is clubs. If you bid 4 NT in the hope
that your partner will respond 5 hearts and instead hear him
say 5 diamonds, you are already committed to the small
slam, as clubs is a lower-ranking suit.

You will want to know the mathematical odds involved in
bidding slams. For bidding and making a small slam when
not vulnerable you receive a bonus of 500 points. What
happens if you go down? You lose 150 for the eleven tricks
you would have made, plus 50 for one undoubled undertrick, plus 300 for the value of the game. This 300 is an
"invisible" asset at rubber Bridge but is actually so scored at
duplicate. This means that in bidding a small slam you are
risking 500 to gain 500, which is an even money chance.
From this it is clear that a small slam should be bid whenever
the twelfth trick depends upon a finesse. I should point out
here that a good player always accepts such a chance,
because the expected finesse may often be avoided by an
Endplay or a Squeeze (see chapter 17). The expert's skill
turns many an even money chance into a certainty.

We need not go into the actual figures involved when you
are vulnerable, but approximately the same odds apply.
When a grand slam, however, is being contemplated, the
chances are quite different. If you bid a vulnerable grand
slam and go one down you lose 280+1250 (the value of slam
and rubber), a total of 1530. In other words you are risking
1530 points to gain 750. These figures show that to justify the
grand slam you should get odds of better than 2 to 1. This
means that a grand slam depending on a finesse is not a good
contract. There is the further consideration that in a grand
slam contract, though the squeeze play is still available, the
endplay is not.

I would like to end this chapter by showing you a hand that was played in an international match.

♠ K Q 5	♠ A J 9 8 3
♡ 7	♡ 9 6 2
♢ A K 9 4	♢ 10 6
♣ K Q J 7 5	♣ A 8 2

My partner, who was West, opened the bidding with 1 club, to which I responded 1 spade. West now bid 3 diamonds, a Jump Shift (see page 49), which is forcing to game, and raised my 3 spade rebid to 4 spades. I have often shown this hand to average players and asked them if they would have made a further bid. The usual reply has been, Good heavens, no! But in actual play I, with my comparatively weak hand, made a slam try by bidding 5 clubs. My partner had painted a perfect picture of his hand, and the singleton heart was as certain as if he had shown me his cards. All that stopped me from bidding 6 spades myself was a slight doubt about the solidity of the trumps. Knowing that I held the club Ace, and by implication the spade Ace, my partner knew that his K Q of spades were sufficient for the slam. So here you see a slam bid without any 4 NT convention, not a shot in the dark, but the result of good bidding and correctly drawn inferences.

10

COMPETITIVE BIDDING

So far we have been almost entirely concerned with the bidding of the opener and his partner. But the defending side may decide to take a hand in the bidding. In the Glossary you will see that the term Defender is defined as "either of the two opponents who play against the declarer." But we can use the term during the auction to refer to a player who makes a positive bid after one of his opponents has opened the bidding. It may happen that the defenders obtain the contract and so become the declaring side.

In this field of defensive bidding the need for cool judgment is vital. The poor player loses thousands of points by making unsound defensive bids at the lower levels. At the other end of the scale, competitive bidding at the level of four and five finds even the good player taking wrong decisions that should have been avoided.

If your opponent has opened the bidding, you must have a clear idea of your object in making a defensive bid. Broadly speaking, a defensive bid is either obstructive or constructive. The object of obstructive bidding is:

1. To disrupt the opponents' bidding, perhaps by a pre-emptive bid. For instance, after 1 diamond on your right you can cause quite a lot of annoyance by bidding 4 spades on this hand:

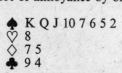

♠ K Q J 10 7 6 5 2
♡ 8
♢ 7 5
♣ 9 4

Of course, such a bid is less effective after an opening bid, because your left hand opponent, knowing that his partner has the values for an opening bid, is no longer afraid of being trapped, but you may well goad the opponents into taking the wrong decision.

2. To prevent the opponents from making their contract, by indicating the correct lead to your partner. For instance, holding

♠ 8 5
♡ 9 3 2
◇ A Q J 10 4
♣ 10 7 5

over a 1 club opening on your right it is essential to make the 1 diamond overbid, in case your left hand opponent reaches 3 NT, when a major suit lead from your partner is likely to lose a vital tempo, and with it the game.

3. To suggest to partner a suit in which it may be profitable to sacrifice against the opposing contract.

The object of constructive bidding is:

1. To pave the way for a part score, game, or even a slam contract.

2. To lay the foundation for a penalty double, should the opponents get too high.

A minimum defensive call may be made at the one level, f your suit outranks the opener's, at the two level if it does not. You should have at least five cards in the suit, and every defensive bid should be based upon the Culbertson Rule of Two and Three, mentioned on page 57.

When making an overbid at the two level you must be really careful. This is the overbid that costs the weak player so much. The reason is that he does not understand the principle involved, and comes in on the wrong sort of hand. Let us take a case in point. South deals and bids 1 spade, and West holds this hand:

♠ K 8 5
♡ A K 10 6 5
◇ Q J 3
♣ J 7

He says 2 hearts, is doubled by North and loses 700 points. After the carnage he says to his partner: "I had 14 points." This is clear evidence that he does not know what he is doing. Such overbids should be based not on points, but on playing tricks. If he had held

♠ K 6
♡ K Q J 9 8 6
♢ 8 5
♣ 10 7 3

which totals only 9 points, he would have had a much sounder overbid for two reasons. First, the solidity of his suit promises playing tricks, and secondly, as he has little defensive strength, any penalty incurred will not be in vain. The first hand, however, in addition to its dearth of playing tricks, has enough defensive strength to make an opposing game at least unlikely.

No Trump overbids

A No Trump overbid poses no problem, for the requirements are the same as for an opening 1 NT, except that a guard in the opener's suit is obligatory. The reader is advised to have a double guard in the enemy suit, unless there is some compensating factor such as a solid minor suit, and bid 1 NT over 1 heart on

♠ A 8 7
♡ K J 6
♢ K 9 5
♣ K Q J 6

You can, of course, bid 2 NT over 1 heart on a hand such as this

♠ A J 9
♡ A Q 4
♢ A K 8 5
♣ K J 4

but modern practice is to make an informatory double first, and follow with 2 NT over a minimum response. The 2 NT is used as the Unusual No Trump, asking partner to show his best minor suit. But don't let this worry you yet!

A 3 NT overbid is a strategic call based on a long solid minor suit such as

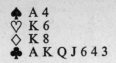

♠ A 4
♡ K 6
◇ K 8
♣ A K Q J 6 4 3

Stronger Defensive Bids

There are other methods by which you can indicate a hand too strong for a minimum overbid.

1. The Informatory Double.

This and the responses to it will be discussed in the next chapter.

2. The Jump Overbid.

This is not preemptive but strength-showing. It promises either a good six-card suit with 7–8 playing tricks, or two strong five-card suits.

♠ A K J 10 8 6	♠ A K J 7 3
♡ A Q 7	♡ A Q J 9 4
◇ 6	◇ 6
♣ 8 5 4	♣ 8 5

These two hands are both good 2 spade overbids after an opening 1 diamond. With these one- and two-suited hands the jump overbid is preferred to the informatory double.

3. The Overbid in the Opponents' Suit.

This is a specialised form of informatory double, and is forcing to game. By creating a forcing situation, just as if you had opened with a two Club bid, it allows the bidding to proceed slowly. It may announce first round control in the enemy suit, but this is not mandatory. Consider this hand:

♠ 7	♠ 8 4 3
♡ A K Q 7 5 4	♡ 3
◇ A K Q 10 6	◇ J 8 5 3
♣ A	♣ 10 8 7 5 2

South opens 1 spade, and West bids 2 spades. East responds 3 clubs, and over 3 hearts bids 3 NT. This does not show a spade guard but is a waiting bid. West bids 4 diamonds, which East raises, and West bids the small slam. Without this bid he would have had to bid a gambling 6 hearts, which goes down against four trumps in one hand.

Protection

Protection is the reopening of the bidding by one of the defenders, when the opponents have shown, by their willingness to play in a part score contract, that their strength is limited. This department of defensive bidding is very difficult for the beginner to understand, but it must be briefly touched on. Unless you understand the principles involved you will not know whether to take action or not.

Let us imagine that South deals and bids 1 spade, and that West and North pass. Before we consider your hand, let us refer back to page 67 where West on

♠ K 8 5
♡ A K 10 6 5
◇ Q J 3
♣ J 7

made an overbid of 2 hearts, was doubled, and lost 700 points, because he found North with a good hand sitting over him. This time we will assume that West, your partner, has the same hand but has been shrewd enough to pass over the 1 spade bid. It is your duty to protect your partner's pass by reopening the bidding, *if your hand justifies it*. You have to decide whether you are strong enough to reopen, and then how to reopen. Let us suppose that you hold:

♠ 4
♡ Q J 9 4
◇ A 10 6 2
♣ K Q 6 5

Your high card points are only twelve, but your partner is marked with some points. If you give the opener as much as 16 and his passing partner 4, there is still 8 for your partner, and he may have, as he actually has, much more. In addition your 1–4–4–4 shape is good, so you reopen with an informatory double (see next chapter), your partner bids 3 hearts, which you raise to 4 hearts. If you had been supine enough to pass, you would have missed a game. There are other situations that may confront you, but I will leave you to study these when you are more proficient.

Defensive Responses

We will assume that your left hand opponent opens the bidding, your partner makes an overbid, and the next player passes. What are you supposed to do? Two factors are involved, your own strength and the strength shown by your partner's call.

After a minimum overbid

If he has made a minimum overbid, look at the negative side of the picture. As he has not made an informatory double, nor a jump overbid, his strength is limited, and he will need a lot from you to make game. Let us suppose in all cases that the opener has bid 1 heart, and your partner has said 1 spade, and you hold the following hands:

1. ♠ K 8 6   2. ♠ K 8 6 5   3. ♠ K 8 6 5 3
   ♡ 9 5   ♡ 9 5   ♡ 9
   ◇ K 10 8 7 ◇ K Q 10 8   ◇ K 10 8 5 4
   ♣ A 7 6 3   ♣ A 7 6   ♣ A 7

4. ♠ K 8 6 5
   ♡ 9 5
   ◇ A Q J 8
   ♣ A Q 7

With hand 1 give your partner one raise. You have trump support—three to an honour are enough for a five-card suit—and about four playing tricks.

With hand 2 give a double raise with good trump support and five playing tricks.

With hand 3 give a distributional raise to game—you have five trumps and 14 distributional points.

With hand 4 raise to game with good trump support and 16 high card points.

To take out into a suit of your own, your bid must be based on sound values—it must be constructive and not a "rescue" bid.

No Trump responses should be slightly stronger than those you would make in answer to an opening bid. For 1 NT you need 11–12 points, for 2 NT 13–14, and for 3 NT 15–16, with, of course, protection in the enemy suit.

After a No Trump Overbid

There is no problem here. You proceed just as if your partner had opened the bidding.

After a Jump Overbid

If your partner makes a jump overbid, which shows 7 plus playing tricks and a good six-card suit, you should raise with two small trumps and one certain, and one probable trick.

After a Preemptive Overbid

If your partner makes a preemptive overbid, you should generally pass. For instance, if the opener says 1 heart and your partner says 3 spades, you will require three tricks, of which two should be Aces, to raise him.

After a Protective Reopening

Your right hand opponent's opening bid is passed up to your partner, who reopens. Your action is governed by *how* he reopens.

If he says 1 NT, give him about 11 balanced points. If he makes a simple overbid, put him with a five-card suit and about 10 points. If he makes a jump overbid, put him with a five-card suit and the strength of a double (see next chapter).

If you know what your partner's reopening bid promises, you will be in a position to advance according to the strength and fit of the two hands.

11

INFORMATORY DOUBLES

ONE of the most useful weapons for the defenders is the Informatory Double, also called the Take out or Negative Double. Perhaps all three names will help you to understand its nature. The first shows that it *informs* partner that you have not a merely defensive overcall, but a hand offering game possibilities. The second shows that it invites partner to *take out* into his best suit, and the third shows that it is *not* a double for penalties.

Before we go any further let us be quite sure when a double is informatory and when it is not. To be informatory the double must satisfy four conditions:

1. The doubler's partner must have made no positive bid, double, or redouble.

2. It must be made at the doubler's first opportunity.

3. The opposing bid must be a suit bid (but see Responses below).

4. The opposing bid must be for not more than nine tricks (but see Preemptive Bidding).

It will help you to see a few examples in tabulated form:

	W	N	E	S
(a)	1 ♡	Double	No Bid	?
(b)	1 ♡	No Bid	1 NT	No Bid
	2 ♡	Double	No Bid	?
(c)		1 ♠	No Bid	2 ◇
	2 ♡	Double	No Bid	?
(d)	1 ♡	Double	2 ♡	No Bid
	No Bid	Double	No Bid	?

In (a) the double is clearly informatory, as all four conditions are observed.

In (b) the double is for penalties, as the second condition is broken. The doubler has not doubled at his first opportunity.

In (c) the double is for penalties, as the first condition is broken. The doubler's partner has made a positive bid.

In (d) the double is informatory. It is merely a repeat of his first double, after his partner, freed by an opposing bid from his obligation to reply, has shown weakness by passing.

Now let us examine the requirements for the informatory double:

1. *Points*. Upwards of 13 points in high cards.

2. *Pattern*. The best pattern is clearly 5–4–4–0, with the void in the opener's suit, and 4–4–4–1 is a good second. The ability to provide four-card support for whichever suit your partner bids is most important.

3. *Major Suit Support*. If the opener bids one major suit, good players regard it as a sacred duty to guarantee support for the other, when they double informatorily.

4. *Preparedness*. You must never forget that your partner may have a completely worthless hand. If some response from him can involve you in a ruinous penalty double, you are not properly prepared to make an informatory double.

Here are some cases to be considered:

(a) ♠ A J 9 6
    ♡ 4
    ◇ A 10 9 5
    ♣ K Q 10 4

This is an excellent double of 1 heart. You have 14 points and four-card support for any suit that partner bids.

(b) ♠
    ♡ 10 8 7 5 3
    ◇ A K 9 5
    ♣ A J 6 4

This breaks the first requirement, as it has only 12 points but the exceptional 0–5–4–4 pattern makes it a perfect double of 1 spade.

(c) ♠ A 8 7 4
    ♡ A K Q 6 5
    ◇ 7
    ♣ K 8 5

A good double of 1 diamond, though it breaks No 2. If partner replies 2 clubs, we bid 2 hearts, showing a hand too good for a mere overbid, and five cards in hearts.

(d) ♠ 6   A good double of 1 spade, though it
     ♡ A 4   breaks 2 and 3. If partner bids
     ◇ A K Q 10 5   hearts, we bid diamonds, showing a
     ♣ K Q J 4 2   strong suit, and, by inference, clubs
                        as well.

(e) ♠ 7 5 4   To double 1 spade on this is courting
     ♡ A 4   disaster. We have 15 points, but we
     ◇ K Q 8 5   can be massacred if partner bids
     ♣ A Q 7 3   hearts. The only sane procedure is
                        to pass. It breaks 2, 3, and 4. You
                        must never break the fourth require-
                        ment.

Here is a piece of advice. If you have a suit or suits of your
own as in (d) above, that is, if you can be the declarer, you
may double with a hand that may not be a good dummy for
your partner. But if your partner is to play the hand, you
must give him the right tools to work with.

Responses to an Informatory Double

As partner of the doubler you are in duty bound to make a
positive response (see below for when you may pass). The
doubler is asking two things:
1. Your best suit.
2. Your overall strength.
The beginner, when he holds a bad hand, wants to pass.
This is quite wrong. The weaker your hand the more
imperative it is to take out the double. Alternatively, the
beginner wants to bid no trumps, under the impression that
this shows weakness. This also is wrong. You should not
respond in no trumps unless you have at least a reasonable
hand.
At the other end of the scale, the beginner finds it difficult
to realise when he has a good hand. Let us reason together
on this point. Your partner, who has doubled, with 13 high
card points in addition to his singleton or void in the enemy
suit, is supplying 16 distributional points in support of your
bid. Therefore, if you have as much as 10 points you are in
the game zone, and 7–8 may be enough, if he has a maximum.

We can formulate a few rules (in each case West bids 1 heart, North doubles, East passes, and you have to respond).

1. With from 0–8 points make the minimum response in your longest suit. For example, bid 1 spade holding

♠ J 10 6 4   ♡ 9 5 2   ◇ Q 7 3   ♣ 10 4 2

or

♠ A J 9 6   ♡ 9 5 2   ◇ K 10 2   ♣ 10 4 2

2. With 9 or more points make a jump bid in your longest suit. For example, bid 2 spades, holding

♠ A J 9 6 3   ♡ 5 2   ◇ K Q 7   ♣ 10 4 2

Though you normally bid your longest suit, you should with a fair hand prefer a four-card major to a five-card minor. For example, you should make a jump bid of 2 spades, holding

♠ A J 10 5   ♡ 5 2   ◇ K J 9 6 4   ♣ 10 6

rather than 3 diamonds.

Sometime in your career you will be faced with this horror:

♠ 8 6 5   ♡ 9 7 5 3   ◇ 8 7 4   ♣ 9 8 3

You have no points and no four-card suit except the one bid by the opponents. What are you to do? Bid 1 spade, the cheapest available bid. *Under no circumstances bid 1 NT.* Similarly, if you hold

♠ 10 7 6 3   ♡ 9 5   ◇ Q 9 4 3   ♣ 9 8 3

bid 1 spade instead of 2 diamonds—it is only common sense·

No Trump Responses

Do not respond 1 NT with fewer than 6 points and a guard in the opener's suit. A response in a four-card major is to be preferred, unless the hand is fairly good. For example, you should bid 1 NT if you hold

♠ Q 6 4 2   ♡ K J 10   ◇ Q 8 4   ♣ 10 8 5

but prefer 1 spade if you hold

♠ J 9 6 5   ♡ K 7 2   ◇ Q 8 4   ♣ 10 8 5

With 10 points bid 2 NT, and if you are as good as 12 points bid 3 NT.

Showing a Good Hand

There is a special cue bid used by the responder, which has received the expressive name of the Kickback. Here is an example:

♠ A Q 7 5   ♠ K 8 6 4
♡ 2   ♡ 7
◇ K 10 7 4   ◇ A 8 5 2
♣ A 10 6 2   ♣ Q J 7 3

South bids 1 heart, West doubles, and East says 2 hearts. This conveys the following message: "I have about 10 points and I can support any suit—*you* do the choosing."

There is one point that must be clearly grasped. In the normal course of bidding, if your partner bids 1 heart, you show a strong hand by bidding 2 spades and a weaker one by bidding 3 spades. This is not so after an informatory double. If you have enough to bid 3 or 4 spades, do not bid only 2 spades under the impression that it is forcing. Again, if the responder bids 2 spades over 1 heart doubled the doubler must raise to 4 spades, if he has the values, a raise to 3 spades may not meet with a further response.

The Pass

It was said earlier in the chapter that you must not pass with a weak hand, but you may hold a hand on which it is right to pass. The pass is a nicely calculated decision to play for penalties. You must be quite sure that the opponents will be defeated in their contract, and reasonably sure that you are not missing a more profitable contract. For example, West bids 1 heart, your partner, North, doubles, and you hold

♠ 8 3   ♡ Q J 10 9 6   ◇ A 7 3   ♣ J 6 2

You pass, converting the informatory double into a penalty double. West may well go down 500, with no game on for you.

The responder who passes the double is prepared for and wants a trump lead. If you remember this, you will not make the mistake of passing with inadequate strength in the opener's suit, and you will bid 1 NT instead of passing on this:

♠ 8 3   ♥ K 7 5 3 2   ♦ A 7 3   ♣ J 6 2

The Double of 1 NT

The double of 1 NT is primarily *for penalties*. The doubler is asking his partner to leave it in if possible. Five or six points, it may surprise you to learn, are enough. Take out the double only with a weak, unbalanced hand.

12
PENALTY DOUBLES

THE penalty double throws down the gauntlet. It tells the declarer that you do not think he will make his contract, and that you are prepared to back your judgment by increasing not only the penalties but the premiums. From this you will see that you must be alive to the mathematical odds involved.

You may make a double in one of two very different situations—uncontested or competitive. Let us deal first with uncontested bids.

(a) *A slam bid*. This has been inelegantly, but most aptly, termed the Sucker's Double. If you are playing against reasonable opponents, the slam is not likely to fail by more than one trick. If you double, you get 100 instead of 50, assuming that they are not vulnerable. If they get their contract, they will receive 360+50 instead of 180. This means that in order to gain a possible 50 you have lost 230. You have laid the odds of nearly 5 to 1 on beating the contract. If the opponents turn nasty and redouble, you have been even more foolish. You now lose 720+50 instead of 180, which means that you have laid odds of nearly 12 to 1 on.

There are other considerations. If you show by your double that the trumps are badly stacked, your opponents may be able to bid the slam in No Trumps and make it. Again, your double may warn the declarer that there are snags, and he may be able to get home by playing the hand in an unnatural way. For this reason the double of an uncontested slam bid is usually played as a request for partner to make an unusual lead.

(b) *A game bid*. To a great extent the same considerations apply. Before you double be quite sure that the double will not give the declarer the key to the play of the hand. Here are two maxims that you will do well to observe in such situations.

1. Do not double if you expect only a one trick penalty.
2. Do not double without a trick in trumps.

These are Kindergarten maxims, but if observed, they will save you a lot of heartache.

Now we turn to competitive bids.

(a) *At the low levels.* It is here, as was said in chapter 10, that the weak player throws away thousands of points by unsound bids, especially at the two level. Even better players, irritated by a series of poor hands, fall into this error. So, if your partner opens the bidding, you must be ready to strike, if your right hand opponent comes in at the range of two. Your hand should satisfy the following requirements:

1. Shortage in partner's suit.
2. Four or five trumps to an honour.
3. Two defensive tricks in the side suits.

For example; your partner bids 1 spade, the next player says 2 hearts, and you hold:

♠ 6 2   ♡ K J 8 5   ◇ A 10 8   ♣ K 9 6 5

The first requirement is most important. If you have length in your partner's suit, not only are the defensive tricks in his suit more likely to be ruffed, but a game contract in his suit, worth more than the double, may be missed. Let us suppose that you have this hand:

♠ Q J 7 5   ♡ 8 4   ◇ A Q 10 3   ♣ K 5 2

After 1 spade by your partner and 2 diamonds by the next player you do not double, but simply raise to 4 spades.

It is also mandatory to have the outside tricks. If you double on trump length alone, you will probably land your side in disaster and ignominy. For example, after 1 spade–2 clubs you wrongly double with this hand:

♠ 7 5 2   ♡ 7 4 2   ◇ Q 4   ♣ K J 10 8 4

Your left hand opponent now bids 2 hearts, which your partner doubles, and the contract is made, perhaps with an overtrick, because you have no trick to offer.

The doubles of two in a minor suit can be employed

somewhat speculatively, because the contract, if made, does not give the opponents game, and, if your partner has the right cards, the punishment can be terrific. For example, your partner bids 1 spade, right hand opponent says 2 diamonds, and you hold:

♠ 6 4   ♥ A 10 5 4   ♦ J 9 6   ♣ K J 7 2

Double! Your shortage in spades makes game in that suit unlikely, and 3 NT will not be made unless partner has a diamond honour. These low level doubles depend on part-nership cooperation. They are to a certain extent tentative—Culbertson called them "light" doubles—and the partner is expected to remove them if his hand is unsuitable. He may be too weak, holding

♠ K Q 10 9 7 3   ♥ Q 7 3   ♦ 5   ♣ A 4 2

or too strong, holding

♠ K Q J 10 7 3   ♥ K 8 6   ♦ 5   ♣ A Q 3

With the first hand he says 2 spades, with the second 4 spades.

Now this double with only J 9 6 in trumps may at times turn out badly, but it can be very paying—I speak from experience.

(b) *At the high levels*. Competitive bids at the range of four, five, and six, demand great judgment. You have to decide whether to double the opponents or to bid one more yourself. This judgment will only be acquired by experience, and cannot be learnt from a book. One piece of advice I can give you. Whenever you are in doubt, really in doubt, bid one more, and budget for it in your insurance premium. For example, if your opponents bid 6 hearts over your 5 spades, and you have any doubt about defeating them, bid 6 spades. If you are doubled and lose 100, when they would have lost 100, it is not good business, but it is infinitely less expensive than letting them make $360 + 50 + 500$, which totals 910 points.

The Redouble

If your opponents double your contract, which you feel

sure you will make, do not redouble without due consideration. A redouble may drive them back to their own contract,
where the penalty that they will pay will be poor compensation for what you would have made in a successful doubled
contract. Psychologically, the best time to redouble is when
there is a chance of your going one down in your contract,
and the certainty of a good penalty, should the opponents
bid on.

Sacrifice Bidding

As sacrifice bidding is inevitably linked with penalty
doubles, it is suitable to include it here. We have glanced at
the problem in our discussion of defensive overcalls, where
the Culbertson Rule of Two and Three was mentioned. But
deliberate overbidding, in order to pay penalty points above
the line instead of allowing the opponents to score trick
points below the line, is an integral part of Bridge strategy.
Shrewdly employed, it is a great psychological weapon, as it
pushes the opponents to the breaking point. Haunted by the
fear that the penalty double may be inadequate, they bid
one more and go down themselves. Intelligent sacrifice
bidding is a paying proposition, but irresponsible "flag-
flying", as it has been called, is not to be encouraged. There
is no greater blow to partnership morale than incurring a
really large penalty. Even two internationals, playing against
two average performers, if they lose an unnecessarily large
rubber, will find in the next rubber that the mantle of Elijah
has been transferred to the other side. The average pair, no
longer burdened by a sense of inferiority, will play above
their normal form.

The vulnerability plays an important part. Pay a *reasonable* price to save a game that you are sure the opponents
will make, if the score is game all or love all. If you are game
and the opponents are not, you must be quite sure that you
cannot go down more than two, even with a bad break. If
your opponents have a game and you have not, this is *not*
the time to sacrifice, except at bargain prices, by which I
mean 100 or 300. The odds on their winning the rubber is
still 3 to 1. That is the point to remember.

13

QUIZ ON BIDDING

In all cases the score is assumed to be Love All.

A. You are dealer on the following hands. What do you bid?

(1) ♠ A J 5
    ♡ A Q 2
    ◇ A Q 10 7
    ♣ K J 5

(2) ♠ A Q 10 7
    ♡ J 6
    ◇ A Q 7 2
    ♣ K J 5

(3) ♠ A Q 4 3
    ♡ K J 7
    ◇ K 10 5
    ♣ Q J 6

(4) ♠ K Q J 10 9 7 5 4
    ♡ 7
    ◇ 8 5
    ♣ 6 2

(5) ♠ K Q J 9 8 3
    ♡ 8 2
    ◇ 7
    ♣ A 8 6 4

(6) ♠ A K 7 6 4
    ♡ 8 2
    ◇ 7
    ♣ A Q J 6 3

(7) ♠ A J 10 5
    ♡ 6
    ◇ K Q 7 4
    ♣ A J 6 2

(8) ♠ A 8 3
    ♡ A 9 6
    ◇ A J 7
    ♣ 9 7 5 2

(9) ♠ A K Q J 8 4
    ♡ A Q 6
    ◇ K Q
    ♣ 8 4

(10) ♠ A Q 10 4 2
     ♡ A K 9 6 3
     ◇ 4
     ♣ A K

B. Your partner deals and bids 1 NT. What do you bid on the following hands?

(1) ♠ A 7 4
    ♡ K 8
    ◇ A 7 6 5
    ♣ K Q J 2

(2) ♠ 7 5
    ♡ Q 9 5 4 2
    ◇ Q 5 3
    ♣ 8 7 2

(3) ♠ Q 6 2
    ♡ K 7 5
    ◇ J 6 4
    ♣ J 8 7 2

(4) ♠ 8 6 4   (5) ♠ 10 9 7 6 4 2
    ♡ 7   ♡ 6
    ◊ 9 5 4   ◊ J 10 5 3
    ♣ A K Q 6 4 3   ♣ 8 5

C. Your partner deals and bids 1 heart. What do you bid on the following hands?

(1) ♠ A 10 7 6   (2) ♠ 6   (3) ♠ K 10 5
    ♡ 9 5   ♡ 10 7 5 4 2   ♡ J 8
    ◊ Q J 9 4   ◊ K 6 2   ◊ A 9 6 3
    ♣ 10 5 2   ♣ A 9 7 3   ♣ Q J 4 2

(4) ♠ A K 10 8 2   (5) ♠ 9 3
    ♡ K J 9 6   ♡ A 8 5 3
    ◊ A 8 7   ◊ 7 6
    ♣ 5   ♣ K Q 8 6 5

D. You deal and bid 1 heart, and partner responds 1 spade. What is your rebid on the following hands?

(1) ♠ 7 4 3   (2) ♠ 7 4 3   (3) ♠ 7 4
    ♡ A K J 7   ♡ A K 7 4   ♡ A K J 7
    ◊ A 8 2   ◊ A K 6   ◊ A K J 6
    ♣ K 7 5   ♣ A 8 7   ♣ 9 8 3

(4) ♠ K Q 8 6   (5) ♠ K Q 8 6
    ♡ A K J 7 3   ♡ A K J 7 3
    ◊ 8   ◊ 8 2
    ♣ A 5 4   ♣ A 5

E. Your partner deals and bids 1 heart, you respond 1 spade, and partner rebids 2 hearts. What is your rebid on the following hands?

(1) ♠ A K 10 9   (2) ♠ A 10 9 2   (3) ♠ A 10 7 5 3
    ♡ J 6   ♡ J 6   ♡ J 6
    ◊ 10 7 5   ◊ K 10 7 5   ◊ K Q 10 4
    ♣ K Q J 2   ♣ K 8 6   ♣ 8 5

(4) ♠ A 10 7 5 3   (5) ♠ A J 10 2
    ♡ 6   ♡ 9 5
    ◊ K 8 7 4 2   ◊ A J 9
    ♣ 8 5   ♣ K 10 7 2

F. Your partner deals and bids 1 heart, you respond 1
spade, and partner rebids 2 diamonds. What is your rebid on
the following hands?

(1) ♠ A 10 9 7 2   (2) ♠ A 10 9 7 2   (3) ♠ A 10 9 7 2
    ♡ J 6   ♡ J 6   ♡ J 6 3
    ◇ 10 6 4   ◇ 10 6   ◇ 10 7
    ♣ Q 10 5   ♣ Q 10 5 2   ♣ A 8 5

   (4) ♠ A Q J 9 7 2   (5) ♠ A Q J 9 7 2
       ♡ 8 6   ♡ 8 6
       ◇ 10 7   ◇ 10 7
       ♣ 8 5 4   ♣ K 5 4

G. Your partner deals and bids 2 hearts. What do you
respond on the following hands?

(1) ♠ A 8 4   (2) ♠ K 7 5   (3) ♠ 10 7 5
    ♡ Q 7 5   ♡ Q 10 8 6   ♡ Q 10 8 6
    ◇ K 10 8 4   ◇ 6 5 2   ◇ 6 5 2
    ♣ 10 7 2   ♣ K 10 6   ♣ 10 6 4

   (4) ♠ A K J 7 3   (5) ♠ 7 5
       ♡ 5 4   ♡ 6
       ◇ 6 5 2   ◇ K 10 9 7 6 5 3
       ♣ 10 6 4   ♣ 10 6 4

H. Your partner bids 1 heart, right hand opponent bids
2 diamonds. What do you bid on the following hands?

(1) ♠ 10 5   (2) ♠ 10 5   (3) ♠ K J 4
    ♡ A J 10 4   ♡ 7 5 4   ♡ J 4
    ◇ A Q 9 6   ◇ K J 10 8 4   ◇ K 10 9 7
    ♣ 10 7 2   ♣ Q 7 2   ♣ A 8 7 2

   (4) ♠ K J 9 6 5   (5) ♠ K Q 8 6
       ♡ 8   ♡ Q 10 6 5
       ◇ 10 6 2   ◇ A 4
       ♣ K 7 6 3   ♣ K 7 5

I. Your partner deals and bids 1 heart, what do you bid
holding:

♠ 5
♡ K Q J 8 4
◇ A K Q 7 5 3
♣ 8

J. You bid 1 NT, your partner bids 3 hearts, and you raise to 4 hearts. Your partner now bids a Blackwood 4 NT. What do you reply holding:

♠ A 9 6
♡ A J 3
◇ A 7 4 2
♣ A 10 4

K. Your partner bids 2 clubs. What do you reply on the following hands?

(1) ♠ 10 4
　　♡ 8 4 3
　　◇ A K 10 8 5
　　♣ 9 7 2

(2) ♠ K 7 4
　　♡ 10 5 2
　　◇ K 7 3
　　♣ K 8 7 6

L. Left hand opponent deals and bids 1 diamond, and your partner doubles. What do you bid holding:

♠ K J 9 5
♡ A 10 8 5
◇ 7 5
♣ K J 6

14

THE PLAY OF THE CARDS

W E can look upon bidding as your Previous Examination, and the play of the cards as your Finals. It is no good getting to the right contract, if you lack the skill to make it. The principles of bidding can be learnt from a book, the play of the cards cannot. To become proficient at dummy play, and even more so at defensive play, you must have the practical experience. I can tell you *what* to do, but it is the mistakes that you make at the table that are the real teachers. They show you *why* you should do it.

To be a good dummy player requires hard work, the ability to draw inferences, to count the unseen hands, and to place the missing honour cards. To be a good defensive player requires all these things, and even more hard work. All the players see 26 cards, but the declarer sees the 26 that are in partnership. He knows where tricks can be won. The defenders, however, do not see where their attack is to be made, and it is their ability to find out quickly their strength, and consequently the declarer's weakness, that makes them good defenders.

The Declarer's Play

When you are the declarer, playing the two hands, you are concerned with making tricks, so it is essential to know that these come from three sources, Honour Cards, Long Cards, and Ruffs. We have already taken a look at all three, but now we must discuss how they can be developed and, as it were, marketed.

If you hold A K Q of a suit, you have three ready made tricks. If you hold K Q J, you have two, not ready made, but quickly establishable by leading the suit. The opponents' Ace is forced out and your two tricks are now usable. The position is the same with Q J 10 9 8. You establish three tricks when the Ace and King have been forced out. This we call development by force. It depends, as you can see, on the solidity of your suit, and admits of no failure.

We are not, however, always fortunate enough to hold solid suits, and we have to rely on long cards that depend on a favourable division of the suit. You should examine this carefully. If you hold A K Q 6 4 of a suit in your hand and 5 3 2 on the table, you will establish the six and the four as winners, if you lead the three top cards and find neither opponent with more than three cards. If one opponent has four cards, you will lose the fourth trick but your fifth card will be established.

Suit establishment is vital in the play of the hand. We will therefore discuss some of the aids to establishment available to the declarer.

1. *The Finesse.* In the Glossary a finesse is defined as an attempt to win a trick with a card which is neither the highest that you hold in the suit nor in sequence with your highest. You will readily see that this depends on the favourable location of a card or cards in the opposing hands. For example,

In the first diagram South leads one of his spades, West plays the four, and the Queen is played from dummy. The Queen wins, because the King is favourably placed with West. In the second diagram the finesse is again played, but is unsuccessful as it is East who holds the King.

Though finesses are generally concerned with honours, this is not necessarily the case. The position might be:

Here South leads and finesses dummy's seven, when West plays the six. This is the time to utter a warning. When the beginner is told about the finesse, he regards it as something for nothing, and does not see the dangers that it often involves. Let us be pontifical. *The beginner looks round for a finesse to take, the expert looks for a way of avoiding it.*

A finesse may be repeated. Assume the spades are divided thus:

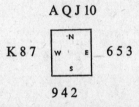

South leads and finesses the ten (or Knave or Queen). He returns to his hand with some other entry card and finesses again. If he has another entry back to hand, he finesses once more. It is not necessary, but South does not know this, for West might have started with K 9 8 7. Let us change the cards as follows:

A 9 4 2

K 8 7   653

Q J 10

South leads the Queen, and continues with the Knave and

Ten, if West does not cover. It is essential for you to understand that in this situation it is only correct to lead the
Queen, if you hold between the two hands at least the next
honour, that is, the Knave, and in most cases the next two,
that is, the Knave and Ten. If you appreciate this principle,
you will not commit the error of leading the Queen from the
South hand in the following position:

A 5 4

Q 7 6

If you do this you will make only one trick, wherever the
King is. In this case the way to make two tricks is to assume
that the King is with East. You play to the Ace and return
a small card to your Queen. If East has the King, he can
take it now or later, but your Queen will score.

2. *The Duck*. The duck is a play to preserve entries. Let us
suppose that we want four tricks from the spade suit, but
that there are no entries to dummy in any other suit:

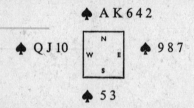

♠ A K 6 4 2

♠ Q J 10   ♠ 9 8 7

♠ 5 3

First we must assume that the six cards held by the opponents are divided 3–3, otherwise our efforts will be in vain.
We lead a small card from either hand and allow the
opponents to win the trick. When we get the lead again we
play to dummy and the Ace and King drop the four outstanding cards in the defenders' hands, leaving the six and
four established.

Declarer's Play at No Trumps

When dummy goes down after the opening lead, the
declarer is in a position to assess his prospects, and form a

plan of campaign. There are three steps for the declarer to take *before he plays a card*.

First Step. Count the number of ready made winners.

Second Step. Count the number of winners that can be established.

Third Step. Count the number of the opponents' winners, and decide which can be avoided and which cannot. Let us take a complete hand:

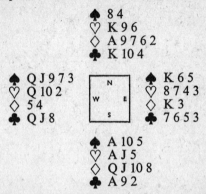

♠ 8 4
♡ K 9 6
♢ A 9 7 6 2
♣ K 10 4

♠ Q J 9 7 3
♡ Q 10 2
♢ 5 4
♣ Q J 8

♠ K 6 5
♡ 8 7 4 3
♢ K 3
♣ 7 6 5 3

♠ A 10 5
♡ A J 5
♢ Q J 10 8
♣ A 9 2

South is playing a contract of 3 NT, and West leads the seven of spades, fourth best of his longest and strongest suit. The declarer takes the three steps. He has six ready made tricks, one spade, two hearts, one diamond, and two clubs. Where are the other three tricks to come from? Clearly, the diamond suit will provide three or four more tricks according to whether the finesse is right or wrong. But if South wins the first trick and finesses the diamond, East will win and return a spade, for West to take four spade tricks and defeat the contract.

Attention to the third step shows what to do. The opponents have four or five possible winners in spades, assuming that West has led from a long suit. If West has as many as five spades, then East cannot hold more than three. The declarer sees that, if he does not play his Ace until the third round, East will have no more spades to lead back, if he obtains the lead with the diamond King. So South uses one

of the declarer's greatest weapons, especially at No Trump,
the Hold up. This is something worthy of the deepest study.

The Hold Up

The hold up would appear to be a ducking play, but in
fact it is a play to prevent the opponents from ducking. It is
a counter-duck, forcing the opponents to take their tricks
when it is not to their interest to do so. Let us consider two
hands, both played in 3 NT:

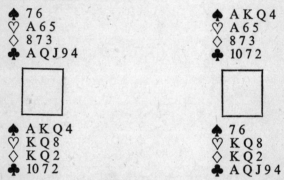

In the first hand West leads the six of diamonds and East
plays the Knave. Be obedient to the third step. You would
have held up with three to the Ace in your hand, so do the
same with K Q 2. If you play small to trick one, you will
ensure your contract. Work this out for yourself. In the
second hand, which looks so similar, the diamond hold up
must not be employed. Why? Because the club finesse has to
be taken into the West hand, and if West wins the trick he
cannot attack you in diamonds. In fact the hold up is the
only play to endanger the contract. You will learn that
finesses may or may not be taken according to whether they
are taken into the "danger" hand or not. If you are obedient
to the three steps, if you understand and intelligently employ
the hold up, the finesse, and the duck, you will soon become
a reasonable player of the hand in No Trumps.

15

DECLARER'S PLAY AT A
SUIT CONTRACT

THE same plays used at No Trumps are also available when there is a trump suit, but the trump suit dominates the whole course of the play. There are new factors to be considered:

1. Ruffing Tricks *in the short hand*. Note the italics. Beginners think they are clever when they lead cards from dummy and ruff them in the long hand. This is just an illusion.

2. Ruffing Stoppers. A trump is as effective a stopper to the opponents' suit as the Ace of that suit.

3. Ruffing Entries.

Here is a hand which will show you what an influence the trump suit exerts:

```
                    ♠ Q 6 3
                    ♡ 7
                    ◊ K Q 10 9 6
                    ♣ K 9 6 5
  ♠ 9 8 2                         ♠ 7 5
  ♡ K Q J 10 5                    ♡ 8 3 2
  ◊ A 8                           ◊ 7 4 3 2
  ♣ 10 8 2                        ♣ Q J 7 4
                    ♠ A K J 10 4
                    ♡ A 9 6 4
                    ◊ J 5
                    ♣ A 3
```

If South plays the hand in 3 NT, he has eight established winners, with four more easily establishable in diamonds, but he will not make 3 NT, because West leads the King of

hearts, and must make four hearts and the Ace of diamonds
before the declarer can set up the diamonds. If, however, he
is playing in a spade contract he will make twelve tricks.
He wins the heart lead, plays Ace and Queen of spades, and
gets out West's Ace of diamonds. West cannot make another
heart because the lowly three of spades in dummy is an
effective stopper. This is what Culbertson meant by a "busy"
trump.

You must grasp this difference between busy and idle
trumps, before you can acquire any mastery of trump
control. It will show you when to draw them completely,
when to draw them partly, and when not to draw them at all.
All hands played with a trump suit fall into three classes:

    (a) Where trumps are drawn immediately.

    (b) Where the drawing of trumps is delayed.

    (c) Where there is no attempt to draw the trumps.

The first class is easy to play. The opponents' trumps are
drawn, and winners are set up as in No Trumps.

The second class includes the majority of suit contracts.
Beginners, and indeed more advanced players, find these
difficult, as they require delicate handling and most precise
timing.

The third class gives the beginner great pleasure. He finds
these hands require no mental effort. For all that, there is
some preliminary work to be done. The declarer must satisfy
himself that the crossruff will yield enough tricks.

If you examine some hands, you will be able to see the
principles that underlie the various plays. We will assume in
each case that West is playing a contract of 4 hearts:

    ♠ Q 4   ♠ A K 6 5
    ♡ K J 10 6 3   ♡ Q 9 7 4
    ◇ A 6 3   ◇ 9 7 2
    ♣ K Q 5   ♣ J 2

North leads the King of diamonds, and West wins. If he
plays a trump at once, the defenders will take two diamond
tricks, a club, and the Ace of trumps. Therefore, before
touching trumps West plays Queen, King, and Ace of

spades, discarding one of his diamonds. By this means he makes his contract.

♠ 10 6 3	♠ 8 7 2
♡ A Q J 10 5	♡ K 7 6
◇ A 10 7	◇ 8 5
♣ 7 5	♣ A K Q 6 3

The defence cash three spade tricks and then lead a diamond, which the declarer wins with the Ace. A poor player would draw trumps, and then play on clubs. If the clubs were divided 3–3, he would make his contract, but this is against the odds. The proper method is to play Queen and Knave of trumps. If both opponents follow you play Ace and King of clubs, ruff the three of clubs with the Ace of trumps, North failing to follow suit. A trump to dummy's King draws the last trump and gives you access to the two good clubs.

Here you have learnt two lessons, the partial postponement of trump drawing, in order to preserve an entry for an established, and the establishment of low cards by ruffing out the losers.

♠ A K 7 2	♠ 8 5
♡ A K Q J 8	♡ 10 9 6
◇ 10 3	◇ K 9 7 4
♣ 6 4	♣ A 10 9 2

In this third hand North leads the King of clubs, which is won in dummy. There are five possible losers, if trumps are drawn, so West first cashes Ace and King of spades. A small spade is ruffed with the nine or ten of hearts, the West hand is re-entered by leading the six of hearts to the eight, and the last spade is ruffed with the remaining heart. Here you see the postponement of trump drawing in order to ruff losers.

The Crossruff

The crossruff belongs to the third class, where trumps are not drawn at all, but the declarer and dummy make their trumps separately. For example:

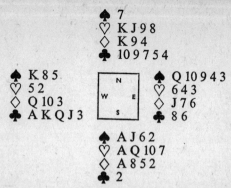

```
                          ♠ 7
                          ♡ K J 9 8
                          ♢ K 9 4
                          ♣ 10 9 7 5 4
      ♠ K 8 5           ┌─────────┐        ♠ Q 10 9 4 3
      ♡ 5 2             │    N    │        ♡ 6 4 3
      ♢ Q 10 3          │ W     E │        ♢ J 7 6
      ♣ A K Q J 3       │    S    │        ♣ 8 6
                        └─────────┘
                          ♠ A J 6 2
                          ♡ A Q 10 7
                          ♢ A 8 5 2
                          ♣ 2
```

South is in 4 hearts against the lead of the King of clubs. The Ace of clubs follows, and South ruffs. His only hope is a crossruff. He counts one spade and two diamond winners, three spade ruffs in dummy, four club ruffs in hand, and the King of trumps. This gives a total of eleven tricks. As he has the high trumps in both hands he is in no danger of an over-ruff. But before embarking on the crossruff the declarer must comply with the following rule: *Cash winners in the side suits before starting the crossruff.* Unless this is done, East will be able to get rid of diamonds on the clubs, and the diamond winners will be endangered.

16

ELIMINATION PLAY

ELIMINATION really refers to the stripping process preceding the endplay, but as it is also loosely applied to the endplay itself, I have left it as the chapter heading.

The alert declarer is always on the look out for the opportunity of executing an endplay or throw-in, as it is also called. Let us go back to a basic finesse situation, where dummy holds two small cards of a suit and the declarer A Q:

♠ 4 3

♠ A Q

With the lead in dummy the declarer, needing two tricks for his contract, gets home only if East holds the spade King. But if West instead of dummy had the lead, the declarer would make his contract, wherever the King was. Let us go back one trick:

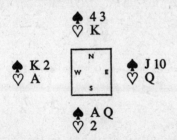

South, or North, leads a heart, and West is thrown in and forced to lead a spade. In the play of a complete hand the declarer seeks to bring about this position, where West is thrown in at the eleventh trick, with only spades to lead. This requires the elimination of any card in another suit that might serve as an exit. Let us see this elimination employed in the following hand:

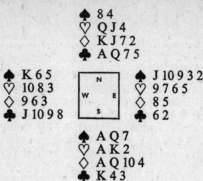

```
              ♠ 8 4
              ♡ Q J 4
              ◇ K J 7 2
              ♣ A Q 7 5
♠ K 6 5                        ♠ J 10 9 3 2
♡ 10 8 3          N           ♡ 9 7 6 5
◇ 9 6 3       W      E        ◇ 8 5
♣ J 10 9 8        S           ♣ 6 2
              ♠ A Q 7
              ♡ A K 2
              ◇ A Q 10 4
              ♣ K 4 3
```

South is in a contract of 6 NT, and West leads the Knave of clubs, won by dummy's Ace. The declarer counts three (possibly four) club tricks, four diamonds, three hearts, and one spade, with the spade finesse in reserve. He plays four rounds of diamonds, West throwing a spade, and East a club and a spade. The King and Queen of clubs are cashed, East letting go two hearts, followed by three hearts, ending in dummy. This is now the position:

```
              ♠ 8 4
              ♣ 7
♠ K 5              N           ♠ J 10 9
♣ 10          W      E
                   S
              ♠ A Q 7
```

South, knowing that West has the ten of clubs and two spades, throws him in with the club, to lead away from the spade King.

When this throw-in play is executed in a trump contract, the additional element of the ruff discard, which allows the declarer to ruff in one hand and discard a loser in the other, involves a change in the modus operandi. Now the elimination consists in stripping dummy and declarer of suits other than trumps and the suit in which the tenace is held. The declarer and dummy must each have at least one trump left. Here is a complete hand:

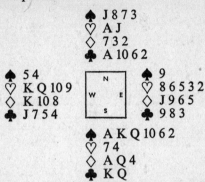

♠ J 8 7 3
♡ A J
◊ 7 3 2
♣ A 10 6 2

♠ 5 4
♡ K Q 10 9
◊ K 10 8
♣ J 7 5 4

♠ 9
♡ 8 6 5 3 2
◊ J 9 6 5
♣ 9 8 3

♠ A K Q 10 6 2
♡ 7 4
◊ A Q 4
♣ K Q

South is in 6 spades, and West leads the King of hearts, won on the table. Trumps are drawn in two rounds and the King and Queen of clubs are cashed. Dummy is entered with a trump, and a diamond is discarded on the Ace of clubs. The ten of clubs is now ruffed—this eliminates clubs from both hands—and a heart is led. This at the same time throws West into the lead and eliminates hearts. West has the choice of leading a diamond up to the tenace, or a heart, which North ruffs while South discards the Queen of diamonds.

On occasions it may not matter which opponent is thrown in:

♠ A 10 9 4
♡ K 7 3
◊ K 5 2
♣ A 10 4

♠ K Q J 5
♡ A Q 4
◊ A 8 6
♣ K J 2

South in 6 spades gets a spade lead and draws trumps in three rounds. He eliminates hearts, and follows with Ace, King, and another diamond, which completes the elimination. Whichever opponent wins is endplayed, because both the declarer and dummy hold tenace positions in the club suit. A club lead traps the Queen, and a red suit lead gives the ruff and discard.

17

SQUEEZE PLAY

SQUEEZE play is the exploitation of the inability of one person to guard two fronts simultaneously. We see this principle at work when two Rugby three-quarters, running together, have only the full back to oppose. If the man with the ball is tackled, he passes, and the winger gets through.

The mechanics of the squeeze are very simple. The difficulty lies in recognising the possibilities of a squeeze, in mentally projecting the play to the squeeze position, and in making proper preparations for it. Let us take a look at a basic three-card position:

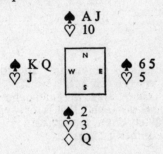

When South leads the Queen of diamonds, West has to throw either a spade, which makes both dummy's spades good, or the Knave of hearts, which sets up dummy's ten. Dummy, discarding after West, can keep whichever suit West unguards.

The essential ingredients for a Simple Squeeze are two menaces *against the same opponent*. These are, in the diagram above, the ten of hearts and the Knave of spades. One of these menaces must be accompanied by a winner, to provide an entry. This is the Ace of spades. For this reason there must be a card of this suit (here the two of spades) in the opposite hand, in order to allow of this entry. There must also be a squeeze card, which is here the Queen of diamonds. At the time the squeeze card is played the victim of the squeeze must hold *only* busy cards in his hand.

We used this word *busy* in connection with trumps on page 94. This most expressive term was invented by Culbertson, who defined a busy card as one needed as a stopper, entry, or guard. You will read more about this in our discussion of the Rule of N minus 1.

Now let us exchange the East and West hands:

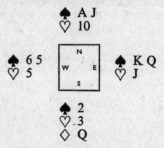

When the diamond is led, dummy discards before East, and there is no squeeze. From this we can establish a rule that when both menaces are in the hand opposite the squeeze card, the squeeze is positional, that is, only effective against the player on the left of the squeeze card.

Let us make another change:

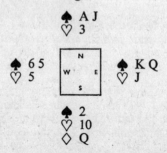

Now the squeeze works equally against East. This gives us

another rule that, when the one-card menace is in the same
hand as the squeeze card, the squeeze is effective against
either opponent. This is known as the Automatic squeeze.

Leaving the Simple (or Single) squeeze, we come to the
Double squeeze, which is a squeeze that involves both
opponents. The necessary ingredients are a one-card menace
in different suits against each opponent, and a two-card
menace against both. With the one-card menaces favourably
placed, that is, in the hand to the left of the one menaced, the
double squeeze can be reduced to a three-card position:

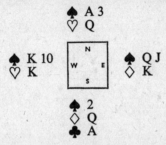

South leads the Ace of clubs, and West must let go the ten
of spades, and dummy throws the Queen of hearts, which is
no longer of service. Now East is caught in a basic automatic
squeeze, and has to set up South's diamond Queen or
dummy's three of spades.

When one of the single menaces is unfavourably placed,
the squeeze can still operate, if there is an extra entry in the
double menace suit. This, however, cannot be reduced to a
three-card ending:

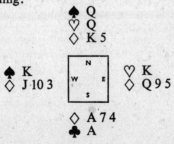

South plays the club, West has to throw a diamond, and dummy can throw the spade Queen. East, too, forced to keep his King of hearts, has to part with a diamond, and South knows that his seven of diamonds will be good.

The Rule of N minus 1

Let us return to the first diagram in this chapter, and make a small change:

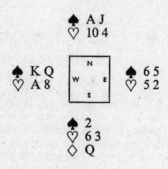

When South leads the Queen of diamonds, the squeeze card in the original diagram, West is not squeezed, because his cards are not all busy. He has one idle card, the eight of hearts, which can be thrown with impunity. In the formula N refers to the number of busy cards held by the intended victim, and N minus 1 to the number of *uninterrupted* winners that must be held by the declarer. To put it another way, when the squeeze position is reached, the victim must hold nothing but busy cards, and the declarer must be able to win all but one of the remaining tricks.

If you have understood these basic three- and four-card positions, you will be able to recognise them in the play of a complete hand. Try your skill at this:

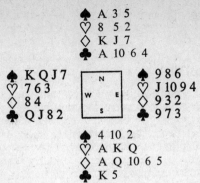

You are South in a contract of 6 NT against the lead of the
King of spades. How do you proceed? You count your
established winners, one spade, three hearts, five diamonds,
and two clubs, a total of eleven. Your only hope is a squeeze
in the black suits. West must be assumed to hold the Q J
of spades, which is likely from the lead, and also the Q J of
clubs (or any five clubs). If you play off one spade, three
hearts, the King of clubs, and four of your diamonds, you
will arrive at the following position:

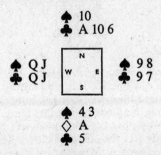

You lead the Ace of diamonds, but West is not embar-
rassed. He throws the Knave of spades and you go one
down. What went wrong? You forgot all about N minus 1.
As there are only eleven winners, it is essential to lose one
trick early, in order to comply with the rule. Where better to

do it than at the first trick? Play the hand again, letting West win the first trick, and you will find that the squeeze works perfectly.

The Vienna Coup

Though this play has an impressive name, it is nothing but an unblocking play, to avoid the humiliating experience of squeezing yourself. The Vienna coup itself is simple, but we will play a difficult hand together, to show you that the difficulty, as with the squeeze, lies in the recognition and preparation for it. Our contract is 7 spades against the lead of the Knave of diamonds:

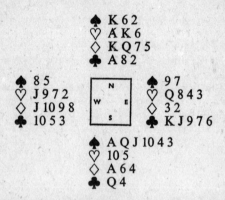

```
                    ♠ K 6 2
                    ♡ A K 6
                    ◇ K Q 7 5
                    ♣ A 8 2
    ♠ 8 5                          ♠ 9 7
    ♡ J 9 7 2         N            ♡ Q 8 4 3
    ◇ J 10 9 8    W       E        ◇ 3 2
    ♣ 10 5 3         S            ♣ K J 9 7 6
                    ♠ A Q J 10 4 3
                    ♡ 10 5
                    ◇ A 6 4
                    ♣ Q 4
```

We count twelve top tricks, with the thirteenth in diamonds, if the suit breaks. But we want something better than that. What are the squeeze possibilities? If either East or West has four diamonds and the King of clubs, the squeeze is on. If West has the diamonds, which is likely from his lead, and East has the King of clubs there is a certain double squeeze. There is, however, a snag. East discards after dummy, and a block in the suit will occur. There is a solution—the Vienna coup. We must play off the Ace of clubs, setting up the Queen as a menace against the established King. There is no difficulty in any of this. The real difficulty is in finding out in time whether it is the simple or the double squeeze that we are after. Average defenders will usually give the game away, but tip top defenders may discard so cunningly that it is impossible to tell. Unless we know which squeeze we are effecting, we may not play our suits in the right order.

Let us get back to the hand. We win the opening lead with dummy's Queen, and draw two rounds of trumps. Now we play off the Ace of clubs (the Vienna coup) on which East drops the nine. We follow with the Ace of hearts. This is not essential, but it makes it slightly easier to get a count, and we proceed to turn the screw with our string of trumps. On the third trump, East completes a peter in clubs, and West drops the five. Two more rounds of spades follow, East and West each throwing a club and a heart. The position at this stage is:

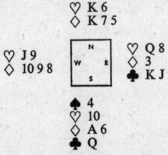

```
                    ♡ K 6
                    ♢ K 7 5

        ♡ J 9         ┌─────┐      ♡ Q 8
        ♢ 10 9 8      │  N  │      ♢ 3
                      │W   E│      ♣ K J
                      │  S  │
                      └─────┘
                    ♠ 4
                    ♡ 10
                    ♢ A 6
                    ♣ Q
```

This is the moment of decision. It looks certain that the double squeeze is what we must go for, so we play to the King of diamonds and back to the Ace, East throwing the Knave of clubs, and follow with our last trump. West has to let go a heart, dummy throws the now useless diamond, and East cannot stand the pressure.

18

THE GRAND COUP

THE coup is a trump reducing play, the virtual discard of a trump by the declarer, because he has too many. This may sound rather odd, so let me explain. If you hold A Q of trumps over the guarded King on your right, you can pick up the King by a simple finesse. But what do you do if there is no trump in dummy to lead for the finesse? It is clear that, if you have the lead in dummy at the twelfth trick, you can in effect make the finesse, by leading any card, trump or not. A diagram will be helpful.

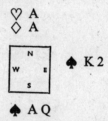

West's cards are immaterial. With the lead in dummy you can play either Ace, and you cannot be prevented from making both tricks. Let us go back one stage:

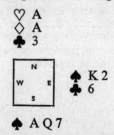

Now, whatever dummy leads, East plays his club, and South has to ruff. This means that East will make his King of spades. You see, then, that South's downfall was caused by having a trump too many. If earlier in the hand South had ruffed one more of dummy's cards, he would have shortened his trump holding, and so reached the position in the first diagram. Dummy must have the lead at the twelfth trick, and the declarer and his right hand opponent must hold two trumps each. That is all there is to the coup. It requires certain assumptions, alertness, and precise timing on the part of the declarer, but the coup is easy to recognise and easy to execute.

You will note that I have rather fancifully given dummy the Aces of hearts and diamonds in the two diagrams above. This has been done to explain what the high sounding term *Grand Coup* means. The only thing that distinguishes a grand coup from its humbler brother, the coup, is that in the reducing play it is winners instead of losers that are ruffed. The play is exactly the same, and you don't get any more for it!

Let us illustrate a grand coup, where South had to get rid of three superfluous trumps, in order to make his contract of 6 hearts:

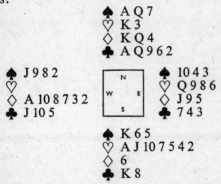

```
              ♠ A Q 7
              ♡ K 3
              ◇ K Q 4
              ♣ A Q 9 6 2

♠ J 9 8 2            ┌─────────┐       ♠ 10 4 3
♡                   │    N    │       ♡ Q 9 8 6
◇ A 10 8 7 3 2      │ W     E │       ◇ J 9 5
♣ J 10 5            │    S    │       ♣ 7 4 3
                    └─────────┘
              ♠ K 6 5
              ♡ A J 10 7 5 4 2
              ◇ 6
              ♣ K 8
```

West led the Ace of diamonds, followed by the two. At trick two South ruffs his good diamond. This play would be automatic with a first class player in this situation. Now a heart to the King reveals the position—the declarer has still two trumps too many. A heart is led and the ten finessed.

Dummy is re-entered with the Queen of spades, and the King of diamonds is led and ruffed. This is followed by King of clubs, and a small club to the Queen. Now the Ace of clubs is ruffed with the seven of trumps, leaving this position:

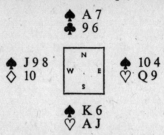

Dummy is entered with the Ace of spades and a good club is played. If East discards, so does South, and a position similar to the first diagram is reached.

19

DEFENSIVE PLAY

DEFENSIVE play is without any doubt the hardest part of Contract Bridge, and the reason for this is clear. To be a good defender you have to do some hard work, which means that the lazy thinker does not shine in this department of the game.

The first problem for the defender is the opening lead. It has been said that, if a player *always* made the right opening lead, that factor alone would make him a winning player. From this you may conclude that the initial lead is a great advantage. This is true, but only if you know what the right lead is, for the wrong lead often gives away a contract otherwise unmakeable.

As the opening leader you are faced with two problems:
1. What suit to lead.
2. Which card of that suit to lead.

These two problems are in turn governed by two other considerations, whether the contract is in No Trumps or in a suit, and whether your partner has or has not made a bid.

At this stage it will be helpful for you to study the following table of standard leads.

When partner has not bid

You hold	*You lead at NT*	*You lead at suit*
A K Q+one or more	K	K
A K J+one or more	K (sometimes fourth best)	K
A K x x	Lowest	K
A K x	K	K
A K alone	K	A
All sequences	Highest card	Highest card
A Q J+one or more	Q	A
A Q 10 9+one or more	10	A
A Q x x	Lowest	A

Leading partner's suit

You hold	You lead at NT	You lead at suit
A x x x	Lowest	A
A x x	Lowest	A
K x x or Q x x	Lowest	Lowest
K Q x	K	K
Q J x	Q	Q
x x x x	Lowest	Lowest
x x x	Highest	Highest

These tables are not comprehensive, and I must make it quite clear that they indicate what card should be led from the various combinations. This does not mean that such a combination should necessarily be selected.

Defending against a No Trump Contract

If your partner has made a bid, it is almost always your duty to lead his suit. He may have risked his life in making an overbid in order to get you to lead his suit. You must have a very good reason for not doing so.

If your partner has not made a bid, it is up to you to make a lead that will be best for your side, not necessarily for your own hand. Suppose that you are West, about to lead after 1 club by North and 3 NT by South.

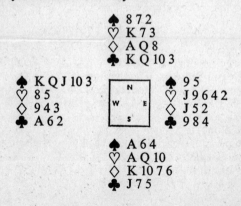

```
                  ♠ 8 7 2
                  ♡ K 7 3
                  ◇ A Q 8
                  ♣ K Q 10 3
  ♠ K Q J 10 3   ┌───────┐   ♠ 9 5
  ♡ 8 5          │   N   │   ♡ J 9 6 4 2
  ◇ 9 4 3      W │       │ E ◇ J 5 2
  ♣ A 6 2        │   S   │   ♣ 9 8 4
                 └───────┘
                  ♠ A 6 4
                  ♡ A Q 10
                  ◇ K 10 7 6
                  ♣ J 7 5
```

If you look at the hands of declarer and dummy, you will
see that there are eight established winners, with three more
to come from clubs. But South will not make 3 NT, because
you have the lead and the extra tempo that it gives. You
have one stopper to get out—the Ace of spades—in order to
take five tricks and defeat the contract. The declarer has one
stopper to get out—the Ace of clubs—in order to make nine
(or more) tricks and land his contract. But, if you follow the
old maxim of leading your longest and strongest suit, you
will win the race for establishment, because the lead offsets
the declarer's stopper and, as it were, upgrades your spades
to A K Q J. This, of course, depends upon the value of your
club Ace. If South has nine tricks without touching clubs
(with five instead of four diamonds), your Ace does not
operate. As it is, you lead the King of spades (the top of a
sequence, as the table indicates), and South is defeated.

You are not always in the happy position of having a solid
sequence. The spades might have been divided

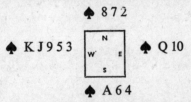

♠ 872

♠ K J 9 5 3   ♠ Q 10

♠ A 6 4

Again you lead a spade, this time the five, your fourth best,
which is the accepted lead in the absence of a sequence. East
wins and returns the ten. The declarer ducks, but you overtake and clear the suit, and again the declarer goes down.

Now with the original hand let us suppose that North bid
1 NT (weak), and South raised to 3 NT. This time you are
sitting East with the opening lead. If you play by the book
and lead your fourth best heart, the declarer sails home with
eleven tricks. To champion lost causes does not pay in
defence, and the establishment of the heart suit is surely a
lost cause. Even if you are lucky enough to establish it, how
are you going to get in to make it? If you are an imaginative
player, you will use your only asset, the opening lead, to
play for your partner's hand. If your partner had made a

spade bid, you would have led his suit. Your only hope is to find him with some such suit, which the opponents' bidding has prevented him from showing. You lead the nine of spades—the Top of Nothing—and allow your partner to defeat the contract.

Do not imagine that all your short suit leads will be so successful, but you will be pleased with the long term results, if you use them on the right occasions.

All the development plays which we discussed in the play of the declarer are also available to the defenders, but to a lesser extent. The declarer, who sees the twenty-six cards of the partnership, *knows* what long tricks can or cannot be developed. The defenders, on the other hand, can only *infer* what is the best method of setting up their tricks. It is the player who can most quickly draw the correct inferences that makes the best defender.

The finesse, too, is available to the defence, though it is clear that the opportunity for repeating finesses must be limited, because the entries are likely to be far fewer. Here is a simple illustration:

♠ Q 7 4

♠ K 9 5 3　　♠ A J 10 2

The South cards are omitted. When West leads the three and dummy plays the four, if you play the Ace, you will set up dummy's Queen. If you finesse the ten, you will prevent the declarer from making any tricks in the suit. This is a correct play—a finesse *against dummy*. But suppose, the suit is divided thus:

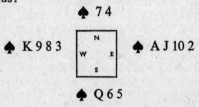

♠ 7 4

♠ K 9 8 3　　♠ A J 10 2

♠ Q 6 5

Now when West leads the three, you play the Ace and
return the Knave. The play of the ten is wrong—a finesse
against partner. It would allow the declarer to make his
Queen.

You will have noticed that the play of the ten instead of
the Knave has been mentioned. This brings out an important
point in Third Hand play. If you hold two or more cards in
sequence you play the lowest. This is the exact opposite of
the procedure adopted by the leader. We can formulate this
rule: *Lead* the highest card in a sequence, *follow suit* with the
lowest. To lead a card denies the one immediately above it;
to follow suit with a card denies the one immediately below it.

Here is a common type of defensive duck:

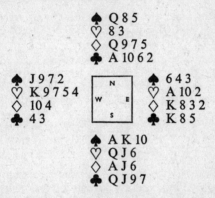

```
               ♠ Q 8 5
               ♡ 8 3
               ◇ Q 9 7 5
               ♣ A 10 6 2
  ♠ J 9 7 2          ┌─────┐      ♠ 6 4 3
  ♡ K 9 7 5 4        │  N  │      ♡ A 10 2
  ◇ 10 4             │W   E│      ◇ K 8 3 2
  ♣ 4 3              │  S  │      ♣ K 8 5
                     └─────┘
               ♠ A K 10
               ♡ Q J 6
               ◇ A J 6
               ♣ Q J 9 7
```

West leads the five of hearts against 3 NT. East plays the
Ace and returns the ten, covered by the Knave. If West takes
this trick, the declarer gets home. But West ducks, hoping
that his partner has an entry and the missing two of hearts to
return. In that case he will take three more tricks and defeat
the contract.

The same principle applies to the lead of the fourth best
from a suit such as A K 7 5 4. If the leader plays Ace, King
and another, even if he has a probable entry himself, he
takes away any chance his partner might have had of
returning the suit. Suppose partner has two small cards in
the suit, dummy J x x and declarer Q x x. After the lead of

the fourth best, which is really a defensive duck, if partner gets in, he still has a card of the suit to lead back.

The leader's partner must be careful not to block the suit led. Here are two examples of vital unblocking:

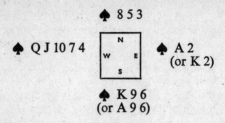

When West leads the Queen, if East with either A 2 or K 2 fails to unblock by playing the high card, a tempo, which may be all-important, is lost.

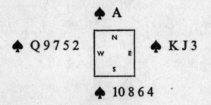

The situation above occurred in a pairs tournament. I led the five against 3 NT, and my partner unblocked at trick one by throwing the Knave. This allowed us to defeat the contract, by picking up the declarer's ten by finesse, when we regained the lead.

Leads against a Suit Contract

Though the conventions observed at No Trumps apply equally to play at a suit contract, the approach is fundamentally different. The long cards, which the defence tries to set up at No Trumps, do not as a general rule operate because of the ruffing element, so the main object of the defenders is to establish and cash winners quickly, before the declarer can draw trumps and get his side suits working for discards.

Against a suit contract there is nothing better than opening from A K Q in a suit with no small cards. The shortness of the suit makes ruffing by the declarer less likely, you cannot give anything away by the lead, and it allows you to have a look at dummy. This may indicate the right line of defence. The lead from A K x is also highly regarded, but it must be pointed out that on occasions this will lose a contract, when dummy has Q x x, by allowing the declarer the extra tempo to set up the Queen for a discard.

Very popular with average players is the lead of a singleton or doubleton in the hope of making a ruff, but they must be used with discretion. At the right moment they can beat an otherwise invincible contract, at the wrong moment they can lose the contract by placing the cards for the declarer.

The old saying "When in doubt lead trumps" is, of course, absurd. The trump lead is occasionally employed to protect the leader's honours in the side suits, but it is most effective when the opponents' bidding has indicated that an attack on dummy's ruffing power is the best line of defence. For example:

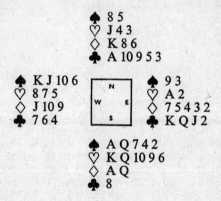

```
                  ♠ 8 5
                  ♡ J 4 3
                  ◇ K 8 6
                  ♣ A 10 9 5 3

♠ K J 10 6                      ♠ 9 3
♡ 8 7 5            N            ♡ A 2
◇ J 10 9      W        E        ◇ 7 5 4 3 2
♣ 7 6 4           S            ♣ K Q J 2

                  ♠ A Q 7 4 2
                  ♡ K Q 10 9 6
                  ◇ A Q
                  ♣ 8
```

South bids 1 spade, North 1 NT, South rebids 3 hearts, and North says 4 hearts. North's preference for hearts and

West's own strong holding in spades, the declarer's first suit, show the wisdom of leading a trump. East wins and returns a trump, and when West takes a spade trick he leads a third round of trumps, putting the contract one down. Without a trump lead and continuation the declarer gets home.

Signals

The defenders must exchange information, not by word of mouth, but by signals intelligently transmitted and intelligently received. Third Hand must tell his partner whether he likes his lead or not. He does this by playing an encouraging or discouraging card. These signals are all variations of the peter (or echo). This is the play of an unnecessarily high card, followed by a lower one later. Sometimes the peter cannot be completed, and the high card is all the information that the defender can give. Here is an example of a peter:

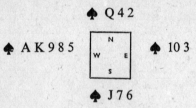

♠ Q 4 2

♠ A K 9 8 5   ♠ 10 3

♠ J 7 6

The spade suit is distributed as above when, against the declarer's contract of 4 hearts, you open the King of spades. On your King your partner drops his ten, a card high enough to alert you. This is the start of the peter. When you continue with the Ace, he completes the peter by playing the three. You lead another spade and East ruffs. As you have another certain winner this allows you to defeat the contract. Without the information from your partner that he could ruff you would not have known what line to adopt.

The peter does not necessarily show a doubleton. It merely asks partner to "come on." For instance, let us suppose the spades in the diagram were divided in this way:

East again drops the ten on his partner's King, because he wants him to go on with the suit. This allows the defenders to make three tricks before they can be discarded on a side suit.

You saw in the above examples a peter with an honour—the ten. This may also be employed with the Knave, but NOT with the Queen. At a suit contract, to play the Queen indicates either a singleton, or the holding of Q J with or without other cards. It is an unconditional demand on partner to follow with a small card in the suit. Here is an instructive example:

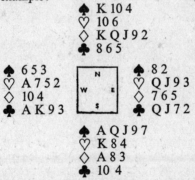

Against South's 4 spades West leads the King of clubs, on which East drops the Queen. Obediently West follows with the three, East gets in with his Knave, and switches to the Queen of hearts, to put the declarer one down. No other play at the second trick will break the contract.

There are two special forms of the peter which you should study.

1. The peter in the trump suit. This shows an original holding of three cards in the trump suit. It must not be used indiscriminately, but only to indicate the ability to ruff. It can be used when actually ruffing. For instance, your partner leads a club, and you ruff. Your trumps are 7 5 3. You ruff first with the five, put your partner back in the lead in another suit, and ruff another club with the three. This tells your partner that you have another trump to ruff with, if he gets in again.

2. The peter at No Trumps in dummy's long suit. This shows the holding of two (or four) cards in the suit. Failure to peter shows exactly three cards in the suit. Its object is to tell partner how long to hold up his stopper in the suit. With an entryless dummy this can be of great importance. For example:

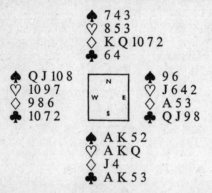

West leads the Queen of spades against 3 NT. South wins and leads the Knave of diamonds, on which West plays the six. On the next diamond lead West plays the eight, showing by his failure to peter that he had exactly three cards in the suit. This allows East to take his Ace at once. If South makes a second diamond trick, he has nine tricks.

The Rule of Eleven

This is something handed down from Whist, which you should understand. When partner leads a fourth best, you subtract the number of pips on the card from eleven, and this gives you the number of cards higher than the one led, which are held by dummy, the declarer, and you. Let us see this in a diagram:

Your partner, West, leads the eight of spades against 3 NT. Assuming it to be the fourth best, you work out $11 - 8 = 3$. You can see the three cards, one in dummy, and two in your own hand. You know, therefore, that the declarer cannot beat the eight.

In this chapter on defensive play we have discussed only a small portion of this vast field. But, if you study and understand what has been dealt with, you will be able to conduct an intelligent defence, which will increase with experience at the card table. This is where the real lessons are learned.

20

QUIZ ON PLAY

U<small>NLESS</small> otherwise stated there is no problem of entries.

A

1. How do you define a finesse?

2. The spades are divided thus:

♠ A Q 4

♠ 8 6 2

You need two tricks from the suit. What assumptions must you make, and how do you play?

3. The hearts are divided thus:

♡ A Q 10 9

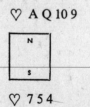

♡ 7 5 4

You need four tricks in the suit. What assumptions must you make, and how do you play?

4. The spades are divided thus:

♠ A 7 6

♠ Q 8 4

You need two tricks from the suit. What assumptions
must you make, and how do you play?

5. The hearts are divided thus:

♡ A Q 7

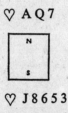

♡ J 8 6 5 3

You need all five tricks from the suit. What assumptions
must you make, and how do you play?

6. The clubs are divided thus:

♣ A J 10

♣ 7 6 3

You need two tricks from the suit. What assumptions
must you make, and how do you play?

7. The diamonds are divided thus:

◇ Q 9 3

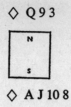

◇ A J 10 8

The lead is in dummy, but you have no entry to the table. You need all four tricks from the suit. What assumptions must you make. What card do you play from dummy, and why?

8. You are in 3 NT on the following hand:

♠ 6 3
♡ 8 6 5
◇ A Q 10 9 4
♣ A 5 3

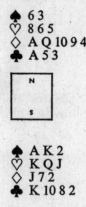

♠ A K 2
♡ K Q J
◇ J 7 2
♣ K 10 8 2

West leads the Queen of spades, which you win with the Ace. What card do you lead to the second trick, and why?

B

1. What is the purpose of the duck?
2. The clubs are divided thus:

♣ A K 8 6 5

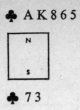

♣ 7 3

You need four tricks from the suit, but dummy has no other entry. What assumptions must you make, and how do you play?

3. The clubs are divided thus:

♣ A K Q 6 5

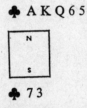

♣ 7 3

You need four tricks from the suit, but dummy has no other entry. What assumptions must you make, and how do you play? What name would you give to this play?

4. The clubs are divided thus:

♣ A K Q 6 5

♣ 10 9 8 2

You need all five tricks from the suit. What assumptions must you make, and how do you play?

5. The hearts are divided thus:

♡ A 9 7 6 4

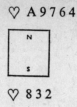

♡ 8 3 2

You need three tricks from the suit, but dummy has no other entry. What assumptions must you make, and how do you play?

6. The diamonds are divided thus:

◇ K 9 8 7 2

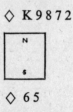

◇ 6 5

You need three tricks from the suit, and dummy has one other entry. What assumptions must you make, and how do you play?

7. The diamonds are divided thus:

◇ A K 10 9 2

◇ Q

You need four tricks from the suit, and dummy has one other entry. What assumptions must you make, and how do you play?

C

1. What is the purpose of the hold up?

2. You are in 3 NT, and West leads the King of spades:

♠ 6 2
♥ K 8 5
♦ A Q 10 9 4
♣ 8 7 2

♠ A 8 4
♥ A 6 3
♦ J 7 2
♣ A K 9 5

How long do you hold up the Ace of Spades, and why?
What card do you play after taking the Ace?

3. You are in 3 NT, and West leads the King of spades:

♠ 6 3 2
♥ K 8
♦ A J 10 9 4
♣ K 10 3

♠ A 8 4
♥ A 6 3
♦ Q 7 2
♣ A J 9 5

How long do you hold up the Ace of spades, and why?

4. You are in 3 NT, and West leads the six of diamonds, on which East plays the Queen:

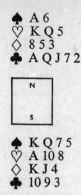

♠ A 6
♥ K Q 5
♦ 8 5 3
♣ A Q J 7 2

♠ K Q 7 5
♥ A 10 8
♦ K J 4
♣ 10 9 3

What card do you play to the first trick, and why?

5. You are in 3 NT, and West leads the six of diamonds, on which East plays the Queen:

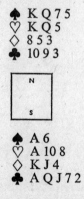

♠ K Q 7 5
♥ K Q 5
♦ 8 5 3
♣ 10 9 3

♠ A 6
♥ A 10 8
♦ K J 4
♣ A Q J 7 2

What card do you play to the first trick, and why?

6. You are in 3 NT, and West leads the Queen of spades:

♠ A 7 2
♡ K 10
♢ 9 7 3
♣ Q 10 9 8 2

♠ K 8 3
♡ A 9 7
♢ A K J 4
♣ J 6 4

What cards do you play from your hand and from dummy to the first trick; and why?

7. You are in 3 NT, and West leads the Queen of spades:

♠ 7 2
♡ 8 6 5 3
♢ Q 7 4
♣ A Q 9 5

♠ A K 5
♡ K Q J
♢ A K 8
♣ J 10 8 2

What card do you play from your hand, and why? What should be your first lead after winning a spade trick, and why?

8. You are in 3 NT, and West leads the four of spades, on which East plays the Queen:

♠ 10 6
♡ 9 8 2
♢ A 8 4
♣ A J 10 7 4

♠ A J 5
♡ A 10 4
♢ K Q 7 2
♣ Q 9 3

What card do you play to the first trick? What are the two reasons for making this play?

D

1. What is meant by drawing trumps?

2. You are in 4 hearts, and West leads the King of diamonds, which you win with the Ace:

♠ A K 6 5
♡ Q 9 7 4
♢ 9 7 2
♣ J 2

♠ Q 4
♡ K J 10 6 3
♢ A 6 3
♣ K Q 3

What card do you play to the second trick? What is your intention?

3. You are in 4 spades. The defenders cash three tricks in hearts, and East returns a club, which you win with the Ace

```
        ♠ Q 9 5
        ♡ 8 6 4
        ◇ A Q J 7 5
        ♣ 7 3

        ┌─────────┐
        │ N       │
        │         │
        │       S │
        └─────────┘

        ♠ A K J 10 6
        ♡ 9 4 3
        ◇ 8 2
        ♣ A J 10
```

What card do you lead to the fifth trick? What is your plan to make ten tricks?

4. You are in 5 diamonds, and West leads the Queen of clubs, which you win with the Ace:

```
        ♠ 10 6 5 4
        ♡
        ◇ A 10 9 7
        ♣ A 8 7 6 3

        ┌─────────┐
        │ N       │
        │         │
        │       S │
        └─────────┘

        ♠ A K 3
        ♡ J 10 9 4 2
        ◇ K Q J 8
        ♣ 5
```

What is your plan to make your contract? What precaution must be taken?

5. You are in 6 spades, and West leads the King of hearts, which you ruff with dummy's six of trumps, and draw the one outstanding trump:

♠ K 10 8 6 4 2
♡
♢ 9 4 3
♣ A Q 10 5

N

S

♠ A Q J 9 7 3
♡ A 7 6
♢ A
♣ 8 6 3

How do you propose to ensure your contract?

6. You are in 3 NT, and the opponents make four spade tricks. On the last spade from East you discard a club from your hand and a heart from dummy, West dropping the eight of hearts. East leads the ten of hearts to the fifth trick:

♠ 8 6 2
♡ J 6 4
♢ Q 7 6
♣ K Q 10 4

N

S

♠ J 10 4
♡ A Q 5
♢ A K 10 4
♣ A J 2

How do you propose to make your contract?

7. You are in 6 hearts, and West leads the Ace of diamonds and another diamond which you win, discarding a small spade. You play the King of hearts and West shows out, and you take a heart finesse:

♠ A Q 7
♡ K 3
♦ K Q 4
♣ A Q 9 6 2

♠ K 6 5
♡ A J 10 7 5 4 2
♦ 6
♣ K 8

How do you propose to make your contract?

8. You are in 5 hearts, West having bid 4 spades against you. West leads the King of spades followed by the Ace of spades:

♠ 9 7 4 3
♡ A 10 9
♦ 10 9 7 3
♣ A 4

♠ 5
♡ K Q J 8 2
♦ A 6 4
♣ K Q J 6

How do you propose to make eleven tricks?

21

ANSWERS TO QUIZ ON BIDDING

A

(1) 2 NT; (2) 1 spade; (3) 1 NT; (4) 3 spades; (5) 1 spade;
(6) 1 club; (7) 1 diamond; (8) Pass; (9) 2 spades; (10) 2 clubs.

B

(1) 6 NT; (2) Pass; (3) Pass; (4) 3 NT; (5) 2 spades.

C

(1) 1 spade; (2) 3 hearts; (3) 2 NT; (4) 2 spades; (5) 2 clubs.

D

(1) 1 NT; (2) 2 NT; (3) 2 diamonds; (4) 3 clubs; (5) 4 spades.

E

(1) 4 hearts; (2) 2 NT; (3) 3 diamonds; (4) Pass; (5) 3 NT.

F

(1) Pass; (2) 2 hearts; (3) 3 hearts; (4) 2 spades; (5) 3 spades.

G

(1) 3 hearts; (2) 4 hearts; (3) 2 NT; (4) 2 spades; (5) 2 NT.

H

(1) 4 hearts; (2) Pass; (3) Double; (4) Pass; (5) 3 diamonds.

I

4 NT (Blackwood).

J

5 clubs.

K

(1) 3 diamonds; (2) 2 NT.

L

2 diamonds.

ANSWERS TO QUIZ ON PLAY

A

1. An attempt to win a trick with a card which is neither the highest that you hold in the suit nor in sequence with the highest.

2. You assume that West has the King. You lead from the South hand and play dummy's Queen, if the King is not played.

3. You assume that West has the King and Knave .You lead from the South hand and play the nine, if West plays small.

4. You assume that East has the King. You play dummy's Ace and return a small card to your Queen.

5. You assume that West has King and another. You lead from the South hand, finesse the Queen and play the Ace to drop the King.

6. You assume either that West has the King and the Queen, or that each opponent has one honour. You lead from the South hand and cover any card that West plays, then return to hand and repeat the performance.

7. You assume that East has the King. You must lead the nine, retaining the lead in dummy, in case East started with four to the King.

8. The King of hearts, to get out West's possible entry card.

B

1. The duck is a play to preserve entries.

2. You assume that the opposing clubs are divided 3–3. You duck one round, and then the Ace and King will drop the opposing clubs leaving the small cards as winners.

3. You assume that neither opponent has more than four cards in the suit. You duck one round and make the rest. This is a Safety Play.

4. You assume that if there are four cards in one hand they are with West. You lead the ten—you must not lead the two in case you block the suit—and play an honour from dummy. If East is void you return to hand and take a finesse

5. You assume a 3–2 division, duck twice and make the rest of the suit.

6. You assume a 3–3 division and the Ace with West. You duck one round, then play to the King and return a small card to set up the suit.

7. You assume a 4–3 division. You overtake the Queen with the King, play the Ace and the ten, giving up a trick to the Knave. You will also succeed, if one hand has Knave and another.

C

1. To exhaust one defender of cards in his partner's suit.

2. Till the third round. If West started with five spades this will exhaust East of spades. The Knave of diamonds.

3. Till the second round. This is enough to exhaust East, if West started with five.

4. The four of diamonds. To exhaust East of a second diamond, before finessing clubs.

5. The King of diamonds. Because the club finesse is now taken into West's hand.

6. The three and the two. Because there are *two* club stoppers to get out. If you win the opening lead and East wins the first club trick, he will have a spade to return. West will set up the spades and make them if he has the other club honour.

7. The King of spades. There is no need to hold up yet. Then lead the King of hearts to remove West's possible entry.

8. The Ace of spades. (1) You make two spade tricks; (2) To avoid a heart switch which might endanger your contract.

D

1. Exhausting the opponents of their trumps, so that they cannot ruff your winners in the side suits.

2. The Queen of spades. To play three rounds and discard a losing diamond.

3. A small diamond to finesse. Then play nine of spades and a small spade to the ten. Finesse the diamond again, ruff a small diamond with the Ace of trumps, get back into dummy with the Queen of trumps and discard the club losers on the set up diamonds.

4. By a cross ruff. To cash the Ace and King of spades early.

5. By eliminating hearts and diamonds from both hands and leading a club from the South hand and finessing the ten.

6. Play the Ace of hearts and try for a squeeze against West in hearts and diamonds, if the diamonds do not break.

7. By a Grand Coup—see page 109.

8. By a dummy reversal. Ruff the Ace of spades with an honour, enter dummy with the nine of trumps, ruff another spade high, re-enter dummy with the ten of trumps and ruff the last spade with your last trump honour. Get back to dummy with the Ace of clubs and draw the last trump.

GLOSSARY

Auction. The bidding.

Bid. An offer to make a certain number of tricks in a specified denomination.

Blackwood. A conventional bid to find out how many Aces partner holds.

Book. The first six tricks won by the declarer.

Contract. The final bid in the auction.

Declarer. The player who *for his side* first bid the denomination named in the contract, and who plays the hand.

Defender. Either of the two opponents who play against the declarer.

Discard. To play a card which is not of the suit led nor a trump.

Double. A call to increase the penalties by a player who expects his opponent to fail in his contract.

Doubleton. An original holding of only two cards in a suit.

Draw trumps. To lead trumps till the opponents have no more.

Duck. To play a low card in preference to a high one.

Dummy. 1. Declarer's partner. 2. The hand of declarer's partner exposed on the table.

Entry. A card which can win a trick and so give the right to lead to the next trick.

Establish. To promote the lower cards of a suit to the rank of winners.

Finesse. An attempt to win a trick with a card which is neither the highest that you hold in a suit nor in sequence with your highest.

Forcing bid. A bid which the partner must not pass.

Free bid. A response or rebid made immediately after the right hand opponent has made a bid.

Game. 100 points or more scored below the line.

Grand slam. A bid of seven, an offer to make all 13 tricks.

Hand. 1. The 13 cards dealt to one player. 2. The 52 cards that make up one deal.

High-low. See peter.

Honour. Any Ace, King, Queen, Knave, or Ten.

Honours. Four of the trump honours held in one hand scoring 100 points. Five trump honours or four Aces (at No Trumps) held in one hand scoring 150.

Honour trick. A method of hand valuation, the basis of the Culbertson system.

Jump bid. A bid higher than necessary to overcall the previous bid.

Lead. 1. To play the first card to a trick. 2. A card so played.

Loser. A card that cannot win a trick.

Major suit. Spades or hearts.

Minor suit. Diamonds or clubs.

No bid. A call indicating no desire to make a bid, double, or redouble.

No Trump. A type of bid that names no suit as trumps.

Opening bid. The first bid of the auction.

Opening lead. The card led to the first trick by the player on the left of the declarer.

Overcall. A bid made by an opponent of the opening bidder.

Overruff. To ruff with a higher trump a trick that has already been ruffed.

Overtrick. A trick in excess of the named contract.

Part score. A score below the line insufficient to make or complete a game.

Pass. See No bid.

Pattern. The distribution of the four suits in a hand of thirteen cards.

Penalty. Points scored above the line when declarer fails in his contract.

Peter. A signal, also called Echo or High-low, to convey a message to partner.

Pre-emptive bid. A bid at a high level to obstruct the opponents' bidding.

Psychic bid. A bid to confuse the opponents, by suggesting non-existent values.

Quick tricks. High cards that can be expected to win on the first or second rounds of a suit.

Raise. A bid in the same denomination as partner's last bid.

Redouble. A call to increase the bonuses by the declarer who thinks the opposing double is unjustified.

Responder. The partner of a player who has made an opening bid.

Reverse. To rebid in a new suit higher in rank and at a higher level than the first suit.

Revoke. To fail to follow suit though able to do so.

Rubber. The series of hands that ends when one side wins two games.

Ruff. To play a trump when a suit other than trumps is led.

Sacrifice. A deliberate overbid with the intention of submitting to penalty points above the line rather than trick points below the line.

Sequence. Three or more cards of the same suit in unbroken order.

Set. To defeat or break the contract.

Set up. See Establish.

Side suit. 1. A suit other than trumps. 2. A secondary suit held by the declarer.

Signal. A play or series of plays by the defenders with a conventional meaning.

Sign-off. A bid that indicates that no further values are held.

Singleton. An original holding of only one card in a suit.

Small [Little] slam. A bid of six, an offer to make twelve of the thirteen tricks.

Squeeze. An advanced play forcing an opponent to discard a vital card.

Stayman. A conventional bid of 2 clubs over 1 No Trump asking opener to bid a four-card major.

Stopper. A card that will interrupt the run of the opponents' suit.

Strip. A play by the declarer to eliminate from his own hand and from dummy the cards in one or two suits.

Suit preference signal. An advanced signal, indicating which suit to switch to.

Support. Sufficient cards in partner's suit to justify a raise.

System. The conventional methods of bidding between a partnership.

Take-out. A bid in a denomination different from that bid by partner.

Take-out [Informatory] double. A double made not for penalties, but for the partner to bid his best suit or No-trumps.

Tenace. A combination of cards not in sequence, with a trick-taking potential dependent on 1. Where the missing cards lie; or 2. Who has the lead.

Trick. The four cards played in rotation by the four players.

Trump. 1. A card in the suit named as trumps. 2. To ruff.

Trump coup. An advanced play, forcing a defender to ruff and be overruffed.

Undertrick. A trick by which the declarer fails to fulfil his contract.

Uppercut. A ruff by a defender, causing dummy or the declarer to overruff and promoting a trump trick for partner.

Void. An original holding of no cards in a suit.

Vulnerable. Having won one game.

Work Count. The point count valuation of honours devised by Milton Work in which an Ace=4, a King=3, a Queen=2, and a Knave=1.

Yarborough. A hand containing no honour card.